OFF-THE-WALL
MARKETING
IDEAS

OFF-THE-WALL
MARKETING
IDEAS

JUMP-START YOUR SALES
WITHOUT BUSTING YOUR BUDGET

Nancy Michaels
& Debbi J. Karpowicz

Adams Media Corporation
Holbrook, Massachusetts

Published by
Adams Media Corporation
260 Center Street, Holbrook, MA 02343

ISBN: 1-58062-205-4

Printed in Canada

J I H G F E D C

Library of Congress Cataloging-in-Publication Data
Michaels, Nancy.
Off-the-wall marketing: jump-start your sales without busting
your budget / Nancy Michaels and Debbi J. Karpowicz.
p.   cm.
ISBN 1-58062-205-4
1. Marketing—United States. I. Karpowicz, Debbi J. II. Title.
HF5415.1.M53   1999
658.8—dc21   99-27506
CIP

This publication is designed to provide accurate and authoritative information with regard to the subject matter covered. It is sold with the understanding that the publisher is not engaged in rendering legal, accounting, or
other professional advice. If legal advice or other expert assistance is
required, the services of a competent professional person should be sought.
— From a *Declaration of Principles* jointly adopted by a Committee of the
American Bar Association and a Committee of Publishers and Associations

Cover art by ©Artville, LLC

This book is available at quantity discounts for bulk purchases.
For information, call 1-800-872-5627.

Visit our home page at http://www.adamsmedia.com

DEDICATIONS

To Bill Kickham, Debbi's most wonderful fiancé and future husband. Thank you for all your love, laughter, support, and encouragement, and especially for giving me the happy childhood that I've waited my entire life for. You are everything I have ever wanted in a man—and more.

To Michael Goldstein, Nancy's loving and wonderful husband, and her two beautiful babies, Chloe and Noah. Thank you for your ongoing support and encouragement of all that I tackle in life. Such gifts I've been given!

CONTENTS

Part four

Part Five

Part Six

ACKNOWLEDGMENTS

It's so wonderful to have the opportunity to express gratitude to the people in your life who help to make your dreams a reality. Writing this book is one of those opportunities.

To Nancy's family and friends, who despite how crazy they think she is, continue to be a support system she needs and values so much.

To Frank Curran, Debbi's ultimate meshuganah and dearest friend-for-life. A million and one thank yous for your humor, support, and friendship.

To Claire Hughes Devine for her ability to provide wise counsel and leadership while working for her at Nancy's first professional job. To Jennifer Gillespie for teaching Nancy the importance of investing in herself—and quality really is better than quantity. Thank you, thank you, thank you to all.

To Dick and Eleanor Grace, much love and appreciation for always being Debbi's second set of parents.

To Nancy's guardian angel, Rose Hart, and her wonderful husband, Jim, who are a continued source of assistance to her personally and professionally. She couldn't ask for better support in taking care of her little angels.

To Sharon Kahn, our researcher, writer, and editor extraordinaire, thank you for being there to complete the task, fill the gaps, and offer such constructive feedback that gave depth and breadth to this book. Your patience and professionalism on this and all projects are so appreciated.

To Joanna Karpowicz, Stanley Stolec, Kristin Lynch, Christine Lynch, and Jack Lynch—thank you to Debbi's immediate family, for a lifetime of overwhelming support, love, and encouragement.

To Greg Kolodziejczak, many thanks for being a trusted and loving friend who continually gives Debbi courage, support—and lots of laughs.

To Fran LaShoto, Nancy's past professor at Emerson College and current speech coach, who, as she did in years past, currently, provides her with direct and honest feedback on her image, style, and voice. To Andrew Rancer, also a professor at Emerson, for helping her to become an author when she cowrote and published her first research paper with him more than fifteen years ago. Also, very special thanks to Sumner Webster and Peter Remelius. Teachers from long ago, but always in my thoughts.

To Lisbeth Nichols, a dear and trusted friend, and one of the most exceptional women I have ever met. Thank you for supporting and encouraging Debbi to keep writing this book, even on days when I felt too exhausted to do so.

To Rena Lipman Lavin, Nancy's dear cousin and friend, for helping her to organize and write a winning book proposal that got our agent, Jeff Herman, reinspired in this project. To Jeff—the agent of the stars—for his ability to see the potential in this idea and go for it. We're very grateful for the chance to work with you and join the ranks of your impressive client roster.

To Carey Madding, our virtual assistant whose contributions to this book and Nancy's business are too numerous to mention. What would we have done without you? Thank you so much for all you do and for always saying "not a problem."

To Nancy Marvin, thanks for being the most wonderful soul sister and remarkable special friend that Debbi could ever have.

To Pam Rogers, Nancy's friend and stable force in her personal life and harried office. Thanks so much for your continued assistance.

Thanks so much to Staples, The Office Superstore, Inc. for providing an opportunity to reach the masses with information so crucial to entrepreneurs and small business owners.

To the ImpressionImpact Production Team, beginning with Nancy's trusted friend and loyal business colleague, Mark Magnacca, who has integrity and wisdom beyond his years. We are so grateful that our paths have crossed in this lifetime. Also to Jane Pollak, Joe Veneto, and John Hersey, our

ImpressionImpact team of speakers and consultants who spread the word on our behalf to seminar attendees nationwide.

To Jere Calmes, thank you for taking on this project, believing in us, providing support, and sharing laughter with us.

Also, to Bob Adams for having the vision in this book that we had hoped for in a publisher, and to the rest of the staff at Adams Media including Jill Ermanski, Michelle Chard, and Linda Spencer for their assistance and creativity on this project. Thank you again and again. A heartfelt thanks to Dawn Thompson at Adams for her extreme professionalism and consideration of our special needs and requests.

To Rosian Zerner, an amazing woman who never ceases to bring joy and humor into Debbi's life. Much gratitude and thanks for being such a special and dear friend.

To Nancy's past and current valued clients and friends for giving her the experience she needed to write this book and run her business today. You have taught her so many right things to do in life and in business. Thank you all for those lessons: Mary Richardson, Karen Bruso, Jay Levitts, Maryanne Uccello, Kim Whittaker, Glynne Kalil, Deborah Franciose, Darlene Robertson, Paula Fallon, David Schuman, and so many others.

And lastly, to all of the wonderful small business owners who shared their off-the-wall marketing secrets with us. We loved speaking with each of you and know that your stories are what set this book apart. Thank you for your generosity and graciousness.

FOREWORD

In the past decade, I have watched, fascinated, as the U.S. economy expands globally and loops back to its entrepreneurial roots. Forging this pattern is the belief that anyone with a good idea and access to new technology can strike out on his or her own and compete on a world scale. In my own business, I have seen this spirit surge in the entrepreneurs Staples serves every day.

This climate hints to earlier times, when independent thinkers seized opportunity with a passion born of knowing that, with hard word and determination, anything was possible. But that's where the similarities end. Today the planet is smaller and more crowded. To stand out in the marketplace, you must promote your business with creativity and courage. You must stretch the boundaries of traditional marketing and take risks.

The pages of *Off-the-Wall Marketing* contain stories of people who took risks. People low on marketing dollars, but high on enthusiasm. They understand that creativity and ingenuity—not necessarily money—can make or break a business. So they blasted through obstacles, mined their imagination, and found genius they didn't know they possessed.

For small-business entrepreneurs, *Off-the-Wall Marketing* is a treasure trove of ideas and practical strategies that educate, motivate, and inspire. It's a book that brims with opportunities fulfilled. It's a book about ordinary people doing remarkable things.

Thomas G. Stemberg,
Chairman and Chief Executive Officer, Staples, Inc.

PREFACE

Why work for someone else?

That question seems to be the rallying cry for more and more Americans—and with good reason. Job security is a thing of the past. Downsizing is the norm. And one person doing the work of two people seems to be standard business practice. The Great American Dream Job that promised security, two weeks' vacation, and a pension plan has all but disappeared.

It's no wonder, then, that there's an entirely new American Revolution going on. Today there are thousands of new businesses forming every day. In 1998, the number of people working full time at a home-based business grew by 1.1 million, to 14.3 million. The 1999 figures are expected to increase by 1.2 million. Self-employment, it seems, has become a growth industry.

However, the thousands of folks working at home and pursuing their dreams are finding that in addition to doing the work, they must frequently find their work, and their clients, much like an actor or a freelance writer. And for many professionals, their training is limited to that of their industry, not marketing. Let's face it—corporate America doesn't necessarily train you to promote yourself or your business. Marketing your own business—especially one that you may have risked almost everything for—requires a different orientation, especially when you don't have a large budget or even a staff to support you.

There's also an anti-marketing bias in our culture, which tells people not to "brag" about themselves, even if they're just enlightening others about their product, service, or business. If you talk to children, they are usually eager to tell you about their most recent accomplishment; however, somewhere down the road, parents and society teach us to stifle discussion about ourselves. As a result, we grow up believing that it is inappropriate to discuss ourselves in public, even if we do it in the name of educating others about what we have to offer.

Having enough money to get started—or to just get by—is one thing. But having enough chutzpah, and an understanding of how to market yourself, make your business visible, and get the word out about it, is quite a different story. Especially in an ever-changing marketplace that's filled with competition.

That's where this book comes in. We have uncovered hundreds of proven and time-tested marketing secrets, and then backed them up with inspiring, true-life success stories. Stories that you can relate to, which come right from the entrepreneurs themselves.

Our goal is to give you the "do-it-yourself" tools to help you turn ignorance into knowledge, inaction into proaction, and doubt into confidence.

Although we hope the information will inspire and entertain you, our most important goal is to educate you about marketing your business. There's no better place to strive and succeed than America—the land of opportunity, a place where hundreds of hard-working people have gone from rags to riches.

Here's to following in their footsteps and achieving the Great American Dream for yourself!

Nancy Michaels
Debbi J. Karpowicz

INTRODUCTION

> **There is only one success—to be able to spend your life in your own way.**
> CHRISTOPHER MORLEY (1890–1957), AMERICAN NOVELIST AND POET

In the new millennium, as more and more people join the ranks of the self-employed, the most important small business enterprise will be *you*. However, what good is it if no one knows about your small business? How do you attract customers? How do you achieve instant name recognition and keep your name out there? How do you create and project the image you want? How do you maintain—and increase—your visibility? How do you become known as an authority in your industry? How do you outsmart the competition and also compete with the "big guys" on a fraction of their budget?

Thousands of individuals at all stages of their business development have shared with us their frustrations and challenges—with everything from creating an identity and positioning their product or service, to dealing with the media and achieving positive publicity for their small business. Small business owners need to become self-reliant in marketing their business, because there's no in-house marketing departments that they can rely on—at least not in the very beginning. The only one you can depend on is *you*. *You* are the product or service that you are marketing, in the same way that big companies pitch everything from bubble gum and toothpaste to cosmetics and fast foods.

How do you start? How do you prioritize what needs to be done first? How do you package your business? How do you learn about the resources available? This book is organized in six separate sections to answer all your questions and to give small business owners the nuts and bolts of successful marketing, promotion, and publicity, in an easy, do-it-yourself, step-by-step program that makes sense.

AN IDEAL BUSINESS-OWNER HANDBOOK, FILLED WITH RESULTS-PROVEN TIPS

Part I focuses on personal packaging, creating your identity, and projecting a memorable, marketable image. Part II shows you how to form strategic alliances among your friends and colleagues to help you reach your professional goals.

Part III discusses how you can gain credibility as an authority by becoming an expert in your field. We'll show you how to become a sought-after writer and speaker, and then a "personality." In Part IV, you'll learn the power of pizzazz by easily implementing some Madcap Marketing tactics to further set yourself—and your business—apart.

Part V addresses how you can give back to the community— and reap more from it than just a good feeling about contributing to a good cause. As we enter the millennium, with a spirit of giving back and doing good, we'll show you how to design a Civic Marketing program that is strategic and complementary to all of your other marketing efforts—in addition to being the right thing to do.

Part VI helps you make the most of all of the marketing tools you have already implemented. At this point you'll be ready to reap the rewards of good publicity from media exposure. We'll demystify the ins and outs of presenting story ideas, creating relationships, and working with local and national press.

REAL-LIFE EXAMPLES THAT YOU CAN IMPLEMENT TODAY

Our book is unique because we not only name and discuss these strategies, but also back up our advice with proven, real-life examples from a wealth of big and small businesses. If you've ever wondered how big companies such as Estee Lauder, Avis, and The Hair Club for Men, among others, marketed themselves when they were *small*, you'll find the answers in this book.

Readers will also learn about small companies that may not be household names but have "made it" by using one, if not more, of the marketing strategies we describe. Wouldn't you like to discover the "make-or-break" marketing techniques that made all the difference for these businesses?

You'll discover a treasure-trove of ingenious, affordable, results-proven tips that come right from the entrepreneur's mouth.

AN INSPIRATIONAL, FASCINATING READ— FILLED WITH INVENTIVE CASE STUDIES

This book is also a fascinating read from a human-interest perspective. It offers brief case studies that explain, in a nutshell, the marketing tools that small business owners and entrepreneurs successfully implemented. The examples given, many of them rags-to-riches, are simple, yet brilliant. For example, readers will discover the ingenious strategy that Barry Potekin used when he desperately needed to spread the word about his new Chicago-based restaurant, Gold Coast Dogs. (Every day for a year, he took a quick cab ride for a few blocks, talking and marketing himself to cabbies who, in turn, promoted Gold Coast Dogs to their riders.) Then there's the case of California inventor Julie Sautter, who pitched her lifelike Curves breast enhancers not only when the WonderBra became big, but at a time when women feared breast implants. (Sautter gave her creation for free to TV stars and costume designers.) You'll also meet Jim and Amy Dacyczyn, a Maine couple who turned their *Tightwad Gazette* into a million-dollar enterprise. (It all started with a simple press release.) Former innkeeper Deedy Marble is another great example; her Governor's Inn in Ludlow, Vermont, eventually was voted "Inn of the Year." (Marble's first successful technique was to write a Boston furrier, suggesting her property as a backdrop for their photo shoots.)

This book, in an up-close-and-personal way, showcases small business people from all walks of life—practically from A to Z. They include Aestheticians, Bridal-Shop Owners, Dog Walkers, Disc Jockeys, Florists, Graphic Designers, Gourmet Store Owners, Insurance Agents, Interior Decorators, Inventors, Innkeepers, Ice Cream Purveyors, Lawyers, Pawnbrokers, Restaurateurs, Salon Owners, Therapists, Writers, you name it!

Their stories are inspirational and fun to read, as well as filled with valuable information that readers can implement immediately.

A MIND-TEASING BOOK THAT INSPIRES YOUR OWN CREATIVITY

We are sure that after reading these eye-opening and often amusing stories and anecdotes, your imagination will go into overdrive, and you'll come up with your own inventive strategies, tailor-made for your particular small business.

DO IT YOURSELF—ON A DIME

The hundreds of tricks-of-the-trade are first-class, but designed for no-frills budgets. Filled with nuggets of priceless, clever suggestions, this book offers success tips on a shoestring. And they really work! Why break the bank if you don't have to?

AN EXCELLENT RESOURCE GUIDE

Best of all, this book is designed to be placed on your desk and constantly referred to. We have included a wealth of resources that can make your marketing efforts easy as can be. To replicate these lists would be time-consuming; that's why we did it for you.

In short, we have designed this book to be a user-friendly, practical approach to marketing your start-up or small business. We hope that you will discover numerous "make-or-break" marketing techniques that will catapult your small company to big success.

PART ONE

PERSONAL PACKAGING

ONe

PROJECT A PROFESSIONAL IMAGE

Business has only two basic functions— marketing and innovation.
PETER DRUCKER

1. Have a conversation with yourself.
2. Make your first impression your best impression.
3. Develop a signature style.

Imagine, for a moment, that you are on the TV show *Family Feud*. The subject is "McDonald's." What's the first thing you think of? Chances are, it's not so much "hamburgers" as "golden arches." Ray Kroc probably didn't realize it back in 1954 when he first saw the drive-in concept of the McDonald Brothers in San Bernardino, California—but those golden arches proved to be a consistent corporate logo, and one that is instantly recognizable.

If there's any one thing that an entrepreneur can do for himself, it's to "McPosition" himself, and create an easily identifiable, consistent image that all customers will recognize—even before they read the name on the sign (or the envelope, for that matter).

1. HAVE A CONVERSATION WITH YOURSELF.

Sounds pretty elementary, right? But just think about what would have happened if McDonald's hadn't created a consistent image right at the start. Let's say that it had arches only at one location and that its corporate colors in New Haven were different than the shades used in Paris, or that its french fries were cooked differently in every location. If this were the case, McDonald's entire marketing strategy would be lost on customers, who would be left dazed and confused. Today, most people only have to see the golden arches to instantly know what they represent—and to derive a sense of comfort in already knowing what to expect. (This, of course, was what attracted "the accidental tourist" in the eponymous novel.)

So what can you, the small business owner, learn from this? That you must create a positive corporate image where everything works together with your product or service—you, all printed materials, and your surroundings.

WHAT ARE YOUR "GOLDEN ARCHES"?

Remember—it all starts with a good name. After all, you've got to name the baby something! But a small business owner has to create a catchy name that fits several criteria: it should sound good; look good when reproduced on paper (stationery, business cards, etc.); differentiate itself from the competition; and, nowadays, also have a Web domain that's not already taken. A great name is simple, memorable, easy to find in the phone book (don't start your name with a number), and should define your unique selling proposition. Staples is a great name for an office-supply superstore. And the DieHard battery says it all.

Here's how to start:

QUESTIONS SMALL BUSINESS OWNERS SHOULD ASK:

- What is my business?
- What is unique about it?
- How do I want my business to be remembered by others?
- Who am I appealing to—past, current, and prospective clients; vendors; media; colleagues; others?
- What do I hope to accomplish?
- How do I communicate myself nonverbally through body language, clothing, physical appearance, and voice? How could those characteristics be translated onto paper?

- What could I do to set myself apart that would be consistent with my business or industry?
- What have my competitors done?

After you have answered these questions, apply your strategy to yourself, your marketing materials, and your business atmosphere. The key is not only to develop an excellent corporate image, but one that is consistent with your business.

2. MAKE YOUR FIRST IMPRESSION YOUR BEST IMPRESSION.

Twenty-something Jennifer Kushell of California founded the International Directory of Young Entrepreneurs while a student at Boston University. Kushell wore a professional business suit to class every day, while her counterparts typically showed up in jeans. Kushell's polished appearance impressed her fellow students and teachers—and also instilled great confidence in herself. "When I wear jeans people think I'm as young as eighteen; in a suit they think I'm thirty," says Kushell. "I have different conversations with people; they talk to me about business. In jeans and a sweatshirt, people ask me about school and my social life. I wear suits at airports—definitely—in restaurants, and always at business meetings. My friends at BU told me that it intimidated them, but my professors loved it. They treated me better. They called on me more frequently and gave me respect. My opinions were taken seriously. People definitely treat you better when you dress well."

Let's face it—you never get a second chance to make a first impression. As a small business owner, you become the embodiment of your company; you also become a public person, which has ramifications. Whether you're running to the grocery store—or running an important meeting—it's important that you create a positive reflection of your company. If you were an owner of an all-natural granola company based in Vermont, customers would expect you to dress in plaid shirts and Birkenstock shoes, which convey an earthy feeling; if outfitted in Armani, customers might not take you—and your business—very seriously. By the same token, a successful financial advisor who waltzes around in crunchy-granola Birkenstocks also doesn't create an appropriate, consistent image.

It's common knowledge that we form our opinions of people within the first few minutes of meeting them; the same is true for businesses. When potential customers first learn of your company, they make assumptions, so you want to market your business in a way that ensures that all of their assumptions—and opinions—are positive.

The key is to develop and maintain a professional image that's consistent with your business—most of the time. That means even going to the supermarket or running errands; after all, you might bump into a colleague or client, right?

The bottom line is that the way you dress and present yourself affects your credibility. And you want to be taken seriously and inspire confidence in your customers, n'est-ce pas?

WHAT'S YOUR IMAGE IQ?

3. DEVELOP A SIGNATURE STYLE.

Susan Bixler, an Atlanta-based corporate image consultant and author of *The New Professional Image,* says that "in business, we want others immediately to recognize our presence as being self-assured and thoroughly competent." Bixler goes on to say, "Professional presence is a blend of poise, self-confidence, control, style and savoir-faire that can empower us to command respect in any situation."

WHAT'S YOUR IMAGE IQ?

An effective wardrobe and business image is achieved by taking your internal credentials and making them more visible. This is especially critical for the self-employed, says image consultant Susan Bixler. It is the most powerful and visual means you have of framing and demonstrating your education and experience to the outside world.

It links your skills and competencies with how others perceive you. It will immediately establish your credibility and also give you a powerful competitive advantage, Bixler adds.

Here are some items to consider every day before you dress for work. Remember, dress to fit not only your physique, but the environment as well.

Women:

Add a jacket, cardigan, or blazer to create a dressier and more formal business look. Err on the side of more formal, not less. (Ivana Trump once said that when you're overdressed, you'll still wind up taking control of the room!)

Consider color selection. Black, navy, dark brown, and deep shades of gray create the most authoritative looks. Red, hunter green, and cobalt blue are also powerful, and add more visual interest. Pastels are light and feminine and mix great with authority colors. They are also more expensive and time-consuming to maintain than darker colors, so purchase with caution. Select high-quality, comfortable fabrics. If the fabric is wrong, the garment will never be right.

Understate accessories. Jewelry should not be overdone. Haircut and color, plus makeup and nail grooming are essential. But again—less is more. Neutral hosiery is the most professional. Opaque hosiery is more casual. Your shoes should match or be darker than the hemline. Most women wear the same three pairs over and over, so quality—not quantity—is important. Check the "walk-away" view in the mirror. We are seen more from the back and the sides, than we are from the front.

Men:

The suit is still the power look, if that's what you wish to create. Add a coordinating blazer or jacket over a shirt and trousers, to dress up a casual look.

Traditional suit colors have remained the same for years: gray and navy. Add texture or patterns to create interest and character. Business casual is generally khaki trousers with a contrasting shirt color. Darker cotton golf-shirt colors will look worn-out more quickly, because the color will fade. Fabric accounts for two-thirds of the cost of a garment, whether it's a suit or casual shirt. Although it costs more for finer fabrics, they drape and launder better, and will hold their shape and resist stains better.

The only acceptable jewelry for a man is a watch. Own two: a dressy one for traditional business clothing and a casual timepiece for informal attire. Shoes should match—or be darker than—the trousers. The belt should match the shoes. Both should be in leather—not vinyl, or manmade. If it's too small when you're standing up—the garment will be really uncomfortable when you sit. Go up a shirt collar size if you need to. No one sees your label—but everyone views the fit.

It may seem obvious, but a professional image includes an easy-to-care-for hairstyle (not mountains of ringlets or a shaved head); clean hair (this is an understatement); a face devoid of tattoos or piercings; and business attire (such as a jacket or suit and not jeans). It also includes:

- Being meticulously groomed
- Being immaculately dressed
- Having a firm handshake
- Looking people right in the eye
- Introducing yourself to others
- Addressing people by their name
- Showing good manners
- Having good posture

Adds Bixler: "Our objective in meeting others is to establish comfort, trust, and rapport and it's not always easy."

Motivational speaker Patricia Fripp, for example, always wears an unusual, bigger-than-life hat as part of her overall marketing strategy to get noticed and be remembered. Her trademark toppers give her a visual edge that entices positive comments from people and thus, starts a conversation. "Strangers who would not talk to anyone else, start conversations with me," Fripp says. Washington gumshoe Matt Drudge, gossipmonger and author of "The Drudge Report" on the Internet, frequently shows up on TV shows such as *Politically Incorrect* wearing a '40s-style hat, to make himself appear as a "private eye."

As your business expands, your business identity will evolve. New ideas, services, and products will constantly emerge as your business becomes a dynamic, growing force in an ever-changing marketplace.

Remember: as a small or micro-business owner (which employs fewer than four people), you are your business. So when you are marketing your company, you are really promoting yourself. Your customers will not know about you unless you tell them. Regardless of the cultural pressure to conform and remain quiet about your achievements, it's important that you talk your talk—and walk your walk.

Gary Goldberg, a financial planner based in upstate New York, did just that when he started his business. Goldberg spent a few weeks walking around the parking lot at a local mall, handing out flyers and introducing himself to people, telling them that he was starting a new business. What he did was so untraditional that the local newspaper wound up doing a feature story on him as a result of his efforts!

One rule of thumb: Put aside any tendencies to downplay your strengths for the sake of appearing modest. There is no place for modesty in self-marketing, especially when your budget is small and the competition fierce! Self-promotion does not mean bragging, and boring others with how great you are; it simply means making others aware of your business and the services and advantages that it offers. Forget the cultural anti-marketing bias that we all feel. To succeed, you must inform others about you and your business! Sometimes all it takes is describing your business in one succinct sentence: "I manufacture award-winning widgets, which are exclusively used in hospitals and assist my clients in achieving enormous profits." Wow! A statement like that is bound to arouse curiosity, which is exactly what you want to do.

After you project a professional image in person, you can replicate it in other areas, which is what the next two chapters are all about.

Two

MAINTAIN A PROFESSIONAL LOOK ON PAPER

Quality is remembered long after the price is forgotten.
STANLEY MARCUS

1. Create the brand called "you."
2. Make every communication count.
3. Create your promotional kit.

Your image on paper is just as important as your appearance in person. After all, you want your business to stand out and be easily identifiable—literally, to separate itself from the pack. However, your image on paper—stationery, business cards, labels, and more—absolutely must mesh with your corporate identity.

1. CREATE THE BRAND CALLED "YOU."

When Alexandra Stoddard began her interior-design company, she took $3,000 of her savings, went to Tiffany & Co., and ordered stationery and business cards in geranium red. Walter Hoving, then the president of Tiffany, told her, "Your clients don't come to you for a handout. They expect to pay for quality and innovative ideas."

At the same time, Stoddard also sought to advertise her company in an unusual—yet cost-effective way. So she had bright red shopping bags emblazoned with her logo and gave them to all of her friends to carry around in New York. She admits it was "an army of walking signs."[1]

Another inspired example of a consistent corporate image can be found at The Blaze Company, a marketing and public relations firm in Venice, California. Owner Marci Blaze had her husband, a graphic designer, create her letterhead—stationery whose edges are burned with a torch to create the burned, "blaze" effect. Says Blaze: "The handblown torch letterhead is time-consuming and expensive, but it's cheap compared to what it brings in as far as attention.... My laser printers have blown out because of the ash. My computer consultant said to get new letterhead and I told him that he should get me two new laser printers, because the three thousand dollars I'm going to spend on printers will far outweigh the cost of my not using my torched letterhead and business cards. It's an immediate visual identity.... My name is Blaze and it worked for me to use it in my company name and on paper."

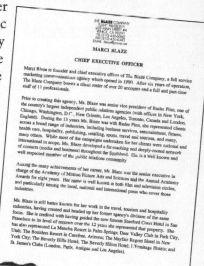

CREATE A MEMORY.

---

[1] *Design Times*, Aug./Sept. 1998, p. 136.

Blaze's last name also lends itself to other memorable marketing. During the 1992 Yuletide season, she had a thousand oversized matchbooks sent out with her logo and the message, "Warmest Wishes." In 1993 the company also donated to the Red Cross when fire hit the Malibu area.

UTILIZE WHAT YOU HAVE.

Blaze is simply following the example of big businesses that spend millions of dollars on corporate identity to make their companies easily identifiable. With a little savvy, you can create a corporate image that looks like a million bucks—only costs much less. Here's how.

DON'T BE SEEN AS A SNORE

When developing your initial marketing strategy, don't think for a minute that plain white stationery and bland business cards will set you apart. They won't! Avoid all generic identity packages that are available at office superstores or through catalogs. Instead, hire a professional designer to create a spiffy image that will not only impress new and potential customers, but make them curious about your company. That curiosity can open the door to valuable business.

First, ask yourself how you want your business to be remembered on paper—you want some panache and pizzazz, right? What image would best convey your message? What corporate identities "speak" to you already?

Sit down with a professional designer or stationery expert and look at all the options available in logo design, letterhead, paper stock, business cards, envelopes, mailing labels, typefaces, and signage, which all visually identify you and your business. Brainstorm and be as creative as possible until you find a match that feels right. Stick to a single logo and an easy-to-understand image for all of your business materials—letterhead, business cards, and promotional materials such as pens or calendars. Consider the price; sometimes a less expensive design can do as good a job as one that's more costly to reproduce (and a smart designer will point out all the options). It's crucial to your marketing strategy to professionally design your marketing materials if you want to be identified as an established professional. If you don't make the investment of time or money, customers may perceive yours as a fly-by-night or unprofessional operation.

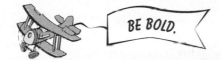

Jay Jackson of Matthews, North Carolina, is a home inspector who has a spiffy logo. It reads "Reed Home Services" and bears a small roof and chimney, as well as a magnifying glass.

Hairstylist Jeff Maul has scissors in his logo. A plumbing contractor has pipe imagery. And a Laundromat in a trendy part of town shows two dancing washers and dryers.

Ideally, if your logo is spiffy and it's placed on all of your correspondence, clients will see your marketing pieces and immediately know that they are yours. One of the most important marketing tactics is to make people aware of your company before they even read your name—just like McDonald's golden arches. If your new and prospective customers can associate your company with specific

LOGO A GO-GO

Your logo should be used on:

- Letterhead
- Business cards
- Envelopes
- Mailing labels
- Invoices and order forms
- Advertising specialty items
- Signs

- Trade show booths
- Presentation materials
- Press releases
- Promotional kit
- Professional portfolio
- Rolodex cards
- Newsletters
- Packaging and bags

colors, images, and a logo, you're way ahead of the game—and your competition. So why not opt for instant recognition? (See p. 36 for addresses and phone numbers of companies that specialize in creating images for small businesses.)

2. MAKE EVERY COMMUNICATION COUNT.

As Ms. Blaze might tell you, every contact with new and potential customers is a viable way to market your business. Consider some of these examples:

STATIONERY AND ENVELOPES

Follow the example of The Blaze Company and avoid plain white paper with black type. Be different! Show some personality! Envelopes in colors other than white or manila also assure that your mailing stands out. You simply have to advise clients and customers that "it's in the bright purple envelope." Make your package the leader of the pack! Jeff Fisher LogoMotives' stationery for press releases bears an image of a train and the words, "Toot! Toot!" to signal that he's tooting his own horn.

BUSINESS CARDS

Make your business card your billboard; if you're going to print black type on white business cards, don't bother. What's memorable about that? Opt for an unusual color, typeface, or message. Make sure to include more than your company name and logo; and describe your business in no more than five words so that people can remember what you do specifically. They will call you if they need your services or know of someone who does. Jill Smith's card announced she was a "Bean Queen." Life Coach Debra Sayre, whose card says, "Clarity leads to success," has a clear plastic business card.

Michael Webb, who writes The RoMANtic newsletter, has a business card announcing him as "Athena's Loving Husband." A chiropractor could put stress-relieving exercises on the back of his card; an automobile salesperson, driving-safety tips. We even heard about a contractor who put sandpaper on the back of his cards. A pediatrician, on the back of her card, could include phone numbers for the local hospital, emergency room, poison control center, even children's services around town. Travel agents could also package their business cards in luggage tags. Joe Veneto of Quincy, Massachusetts, is a travel consultant with a memorable one-fold business card. The front shows a suitcase, and it opens up to resemble a luggage interior. Seth Goldman's card refers to him as a "TeaEO" for his tea company. The creator of Rainforest Cafe has a bird-shaped business card.

The
RoMANtic

Michael Webb
*Athena's Loving Husband,
Author and Romance Expert*

(919) 462-0900 Office
(919) 461-6333 Fax
romantic@aol.com

(888) 4ROMANTIC
toll-free order line

PO Box 1567, Cary NC 27512

HONEST TEA

SETH GOLDMAN
PRESIDENT & TeaEO

4948 St. Elmo Avenue
Suite 304
Bethesda, MD 20814
301.652.3556
Fax 301.652.3557
seth@honestea.com
www.honestea.com

BETTER BUSINESS CARD IDEAS

Whatever you do, make your business card a conversation piece—something that will attract attention, get your business noticed, and make it memorable. How about these ideas?

- Create cards that are bigger or smaller than the traditional size.
- Use creative edging; tailors could alter theirs with pinking shears.

- Try texturizing your card with embossing or foil stamping.
- Leave room in the design to attach real objects to your card: bandages (for doctors); dental floss (dentists); toothpicks (caterers); buttons (seamstresses); bobby pin (hairdressers).
- Use a rich-looking paper stock.
- Design a card with a fold, to create a mini-brochure.

ROLODEX CARDS

If done right, this item may even replace the necessity of a business card. Even though much of the world is on the Internet, many professionals—especially the media—still find their sources through a Rolodex card. Make the tab an attention-getting color that will stand out in the sea of cards, and add sparkling copy—something like "Vital Names and Numbers" or "Chicago's Best Plumber" instead of just your business name.

POSTCARDS

Those with a catchy message require cheaper postage than business envelopes, and are yet another way to make clients and customers aware of your business; just make sure they're not in bland, boring white.

T-SHIRTS

Add your logo and give them to friends and family to make them walking billboards. Jeff Fisher LogoMotives does this, with great success!

LABELS

Make yours memorable with a special message under your name, or a special design in an unusual color. Larry Winget, an "irrational motivational speaker," uses his offbeat photo.

Larry Winget
1362 East 26th Place, Tulsa Oklahoma 74114
918.745.6606 • 800.749.4597 • FAX 918.747.3185
ungawaguy @ aol.com   www.larrywinget.com

NEWSLETTERS

Make it convey all the good things about your business, from the color and design to the content. A great title also helps. Boston comedienne and humor writer, Carol Ann Small, has plans for her own corporate newsletter about her business. She has the perfect name for it: Small Talk. Peter Lawton, a certified Home Improvement Contractor in Worcester, Massachusetts, sends out a newsletter that resembles a set of blueprints. Other distinctive newsletters: The RoMANtic, a mini-book on keeping love alive, and Pawn Bulletin, which is a marketing tool for the Empire Loan pawnshop.

Newsletters offer three distinct advantages: They offer timely information and position you as an expert. Second, since they offer information—not advertising—they are likely to be read. And third, because they are distributed regularly to clients, prospects, colleagues, vendors, and the media, newsletters let you keep in touch with your market on an ongoing basis. They are also an excellent replacement for brochures, which usually become obsolete all too soon.

In some cases you can include a clip-out order form for products your business offers. But remember, the focus of your newsletter is to tell, not sell.

A NEWSLETTER SHOULD TELL, NOT SELL.

Easy to produce, a newsletter simply requires writing, design, layout, production, and mailing. It can be as simple as a single-page with black ink printed on white paper, or a full-color, multipaged, saddle-stitched mini-magazine.

INVOICES
A bill is a bill is a bill... Or is it? Use yours to send reprints of articles about you and to notify customers of current achievements.

PACKAGING AND BAGS

Use the same color as your letterhead, and simply add your business label to the front. If you can afford to, have your designer whip up a dazzling design using your logo.

BROCHURES

Don't do it! By the time they're printed, costing you a small fortune, they will probably be obsolete. Worse, some brochures only tell how great a company is—making them a throwaway item. Better to create a promotional kit, which you'll learn about in a minute. If you must print a brochure, make it a "keeper" by offering information and tips that are valuable to the reader. Likewise for catalogs. For example, any small business owner could ask a local organizing expert to write a few articles about "How to organize a home office," and intersperse the tips throughout. You need to determine how you will specifically use your brochure or catalog. If it doesn't have at least five purposes, don't print it! Ask yourself if you can

- Send it to the media
- Send it to potential customers
- Send it to past clients
- Include it in your invoices to current customers
- Use it in a special mailing to current customers
- Hand it out to vendors
- Mail it to colleagues
- Include it with giveaways at public appearances

Whatever you do, make sure your promotional materials have pizzazz.

Remember Jennifer Kushell? While still a student at Boston University, she and two partners founded the International Directory of Young Entrepreneurs. "We were three kids…who started an international company. We had to come up with a lot of tricks to make our company look more substantial than it was," says Kushell. "So we invested a lot in the beginning on marketing materials. Anything that we could show others that would look impressive, such as foil-embossed brochures. The reaction was amazing. People gave us respect instantly. They expected that we were older and had more experience," Kushell adds. She says that her brochures also contained the tag line, "The #1 Resource in the World for Young Entrepreneurs." "People really liked that," says Kushell. "It made us sound really big."

3. CREATE YOUR PROMOTIONAL KIT. PACK UP YOUR POSITIVES IN YOUR PROMOTIONAL KIT AND SMILE, SMILE, SMILE

One of the most important ways to present yourself on paper is through your promotional kit. A promotional kit is invaluable, as it not only tells your up-to-the-minute business story, it's also cost-effective, flexible, and easily customized for prospects, clients, and the press.

It usually consists of a two-pocket folder that holds a wealth of information about your business and can be mailed or handed out. To avoid the eighth-grade book-report look, attach to the front your business label with its logo. You should also consider having your logo printed right on the folders, whose color should match that of your corporate identity. Your graphic designer or trusted printer can help you with these.

Your promotional kit should include information that reflects you and your business in a positive light. The contents can include:

Tova Borgnine
Executive Summary

Tova's passion for beauty and elegance formed the foundation of what has now become a direct marketing Cinderella story. Along with her mantra: "It can be done!" she has transformed her dreams into a multi-million dollar corporation now positioned as an international presence in the beauty industry.

During her early twenties, Tova received her initial exposure to the inner workings of the cosmetics business in Manhattan while working as an actress. The subsequent success of her East Coast boutique named "Tova's Touch" led her to Las Vegas where she became a highly regarded make up artist. She found the desert climate caused many of her clients to suffer from skin problems due to lack of hydration. Tova began her quest for the ultimate botanical skin care treatment when a client introduced her to an obscure Aztec cactus based facial masque.

Tova pioneered personalized direct mail/telephone sales and through the storms of operating her newly formed organization anticipated market trends. Today, she hosts the highly popular QVC program "Beauty by Tova". In December of 1997 she broke all previous sales figures on QVC with the sell through of 60,000 of her special four-piece fragrance collection gift sets in record time and in the process overloaded QVC's extensive phone system. Tova is now so popular that she appears on multiple hour shows every 6 weeks. Her Signature Fragrance alone has sold over 2,500,000 units.

Tova's "Body Mind and Spirit" salon in Beverly Hills enjoys an elegantly upbeat atmosphere catering to many Hollywood celebrities. Despite her hectic schedule, Tova insists on maintaining a personal touch with her customers.

Her recently published book was released by Putnam in mid October of 1997. She recounts the trials and tribulations of maintaining a balanced and loving marriage while pursuing her career and offers advice on "Being Happily Married Forever".

Tova remains active with philanthropic organizations such as the Susan G. Koman Breast Cancer Foundation. She sponsors an educational fellowship program with the Olfactory Research Fund where she is an active board member. She also serves on the Boards of Junior Achievement and the American Scandinavian Foundation.

THE TOVA CORPORATION

192 North Canon Drive, Beverly Hills, California 90210

FOR IMMEDIATE RELEASE

TOVA NIGHTS WINS WOMEN'S FRAGRANCE INTRODUCTION AWARD
AT THE 26th ANNUAL FIFI AWARDS

New York, June 2nd 1998

The Tova Corporation is very pleased to announce that our newest fragrance, Tova Nights was awarded the International Fragrance Foundation's FIFI award on June 2nd. Sixteen hundred industry leaders participated in the Gala event at the Lincoln Center for the Performing Arts in New York to celebrate the best in the fragrance business. We launched Tova Nights in late June of 1997 and have received a phenomenal response from our friends both inside and outside the industry.

The Fragrance Foundation was established in 1949 by six industry mavericks affiliated with Elizabeth Arden, Coty, Guerlain, Helena Rubinstein, Chanel and Parfums Weil, to develop educational programs about the importance and pleasures of fragrance. Today America is the largest fragrance market in the world and The Fragrance Foundation has become an international source for historic, cultural, scientific and industry related materials.

Tova Nights won the award for 1997 Women's Fragrance Introduction of the Year in Non-Store Venues. Accepting the award from presenters Kenny Rogers and Faye Dunaway, Tova thanked Margaret Martin, a QVC viewer who inspired Tova Nights by confessing that Tova's fragrances led her to have a "Tova Night" with her husband.

- ☑ Your biography (written in the third person, in paragraph form)
- ☑ Background/company history (include the qualities that make your business unique and personal anecdotes about how you decided to start the business)
- ☑ Press release
- ☑ List of services/products
- ☑ Product information sheet
- ☑ Client testimonials and endorsements
- ☑ List of client references, with addresses and phone numbers
- ☑ Client list
- ☑ Headshot (Hire a professional makeup artist, hairdresser, and photographer, and dress appropriately. Jackets project authority and are a good choice; avoid patterned clothing. For details, see Chapter 19, "Make Your Interview Memorable.")
- ☑ Reprints of articles written about your business, or in which you are quoted
- ☑ Reprints of articles about your business/industry that you have written
- ☑ Advertising reprints
- ☑ Newsletter
- ☑ Question-and-answer interview (especially useful for industries or products that aren't easily explained)
- ☑ Pitch letter
- ☑ Premiums (The kit for a Boston-area hair salon features custom-designed chocolate bars with specially made labels with the message, "How sweet it is to visit Leon & Co." On the back is a listing of the salon's recent magazine publicity.)

Not all of these items belong in your promotional kit all of the time. For instance, if you're mailing the package to a prospective client, you may want to remove the press release and photos of yourself. But that's the advantage of a promotional kit over a brochure—it adapts easily to your needs. (See p. 36 for the addresses and phone numbers of photo reproduction houses that will be helpful in assembling promotional kits and portfolios.)

CUSTOMIZE YOUR PROMOTIONAL KIT.

THE PERFECT PORTFOLIO

In addition to the promotional kit, every business owner needs a professional portfolio that documents his or her accomplishments. It's similar to the promotional kit, except that your portfolio consists of a three-ring binder with plastic inserts to protect your documents. Invest in a leather binder that exudes class and credibility; you can also personalize the cover to suit your needs. We know, in fact, of an interior designer/artist who covered his in attention-getting fake fur! Consider this your "master" for storing high-quality copies; stash your original documents in a separate place for safekeeping. Your portfolio also stays with you—or within your office. You might place it in the waiting room to inform new clients about your business. Or you can bring it to meetings with prospects, clients, investors, venture capitalists, and the media.

AN INTERIOR DESIGNER COVERED HIS PORTFOLIO IN FAKE FUR.

The first step in assembling your portfolio is to document and record all of your work and visually present the results achieved. Save originals of reports, proposals, research findings, and press clippings. Remember to use a camera to record work-related events that can't be saved on paper. For instance, if you're an interior decorator, take before-and-after pictures or videos. If you host an open house, record it on videotape. Save letters from satisfied customers, plus special certifications and awards. Make sure to also keep files of testimonials. Like those in your promotional kit, pages can be added or removed, depending on whom you're trying to impress.

HOW TO DEVELOP A PROFESSIONAL PORTFOLIO

A professional portfolio is easy to assemble. Here's how:

1. *Invest in a three-ring binder with protective sheets.* Purchase a high-quality binder made of leather, if possible, and waterproof protective pages to show off your work and replenish with updated material.

2. *Save all of the work you value.* Never, ever toss a proposal that took you two weeks to write, a research report you completed for a client, or a certificate received. You'll never know when you might need them. Over time, you can discard and update irrelevant information.

3. *Keep a file on your desk and add to it regularly.* Feed a file folder on a weekly basis, with notes of upcoming projects, photographs to be inserted, and words of praise from clients, vendors, and colleagues. Each month, review your file and add important items to your portfolio.

4. *Request letters and testimonials.* Don't be shy when clients or customers praise you. Ask them to put it in writing by saying something like, "Gee, Jim, I'm glad you're so pleased with the project. I'm updating my marketing materials and would like to include something from you in writing. Would you mind putting your statements in a letter for me?" Chances are, he or she will be happy to oblige. If they forget, make it easy for them by writing a testimonial letter and faxing it to them for their approval. Request their letterhead and—Voila!—you've got an

instant testimonial. A third-party endorsement, especially from a well known broadcaster, celebrity, or politician, offers more validation and credibility than a full-page ad in the *New York Times*.

You can also generate testimonials after you've completed a sale. Just send a thank-you note, include your phone number, and request feedback. If your customers are celebrities, all the better; you can frame their testimonial next to their picture. Some celebrities might even write the testimonial on their black-and-white headshot, which you can hang in a well traveled area of your business. Restaurants do it all the time!

5. *Carry a camera with you to document events.* When Nancy Michaels had a chance meeting with the late Og Mandino, the best-selling author of *The Greatest Salesman in the World*, she asked if he would pose with her for a photograph. Nancy had her camera in tow, but it needed new batteries. Learn from her mistake—don't ever miss an opportunity to capture a magic moment on film! (Afterward, Michaels sent Mandino some complimentary marketing materials, and he responded with a thank-you note. Soon after, Mandino died—but Michaels has the letter framed and prominently placed in her office.)

If you find it difficult to translate your particular business into a portfolio, break down what you do into current and completed projects. For example, if you wish to open a second restaurant and are seeking financial backers, pull together some sample menus and photographs of meals at functions you have served. Include original copies of letters from satisfied customers, as well as a list of references with phone numbers and addresses.

Your portfolio should also include:

- Headshot
- Photo of your business/employees
- Biography

- List of services/products
- Professional marketing materials
- Client testimonials

SEPARATE YOURSELF FROM THE PACK.

Your portfolio is a state-of-the-art document of your professional accomplishments. The cost is minimal, but the results can be dramatic. Too few businesses and individuals use portfolios to tangibly demonstrate their services to prospective clients and customers.

The bottom line is to ask yourself objectively: "Do I look good on paper?" It's also smart to ask your closest friends and colleagues for feedback.

If necessary, hire someone to write your biography and other materials. You can contact writers through the National Writers Union, which has a Job Bank that will post your job listing for free; and the American Society of Journalists and Authors, which, for a small fee, will match your job description to a qualified writer through its Dial-A-Writer service (see p. 36 for addresses and phone numbers). Also, check with colleges and universities that offer communications/journalism courses; you might find a student who could also do an excellent job. The alumni office might even post a job listing for you. Contact teachers of adult education writing classes in your area and on-staff reporters at your local newspaper to see if they do any freelance work.

HIRE A WRITER!

ThREe

DRESS YOUR SURROUNDINGS TO IMPRESS

Aesthetics, like sexual selection, make life lovely and wonderful, fill it with new forms, and give it progress, and variety and change.
OSCAR WILDE, "THE CRITIC AS ARTIST," *INTENTIONS*, 1891

1. Make smart, not expensive, choices.
2. Create great atmosphere with customer service.
3. Imitate the "Top Guns."

After your personal-and-professional acts are together, it's smart to put your house in order as well. It's essential to go the extra mile and create the perception of great success, especially when you're on your way up.

Companies spend billions of dollars annually on TV and radio spots, billboards, direct mail, print advertising, promotional events, and more—all in the hope and expectation that their message will stand out from the crowd. Does your business also need to market itself? Of course! But you can do it on a shoestring budget and still achieve positive results.

You don't have to spend a bundle to effectively promote your business. You just want it to look that way—and there's nothing wrong with that.

1. MAKE SMART, NOT EXPENSIVE, CHOICES.

Manicurist Gerri Civitano knows all about projecting a successful image. She adopted a very smart tactic on her very first day of business, when women visited her home in New Rochelle, New York, to have their nails sculptured. Civitano didn't want her first customer to realize that she was just that— her first!—and so Civitano ingeniously went about making her home look like a busy place of business. Among other things, she poured coffee into five different coffee cups, and added different-colored lipstick imprints on each, to give the impression that numerous customers had already been to her home. It gave her the "image" of success before she actually achieved it. Today, the perception has become a reality; Civitano has a posh new business location in Scarsdale, complete with the "at-home" surroundings that she became famous for. She also made it to QVC, where she sells her 100 percent organic nail powder that is an alternative to acrylic nails.

Other surroundings can also be used to market yourself. Don't overlook these small-but-effective steps.

Points to remember:

- Be creative in your marketing.
- Make yourself appear more successful.
- Fake it until you make it.

WINDOW SPACE

Use your windows to gain attention and increase your visibility. Display reprints of articles that have been written about your business so that people passing by will read about your business and any positive recognition it has received. Dress up your windows with displays! Department stores do it, and every Christmas they attract throngs of visitors. Videotape your latest ad, put it on a loop tape that plays continuously, and place it out front where everyone can see it.

Salon owner Paul Milea in Fayetteville, New York, used his windows to great advantage. He took out ads in the local paper and placed signs in his salon's windows that said, "Watch these windows. Your friends and neighbors may be appearing soon." Then, while making over several clients, he took their before-and-after pictures, and framed and covered them. Next, he placed the posters on easels in the windows, where they remained wrapped for two weeks. "People would come up to me all the time and say, 'What's under the paper?' It was driving everyone crazy," Milea says. In a period of every four days to heighten the suspense, Milea unveiled the dramatic before-and-after makeover pictures. The promotion attracted new clients and retail sales soared. Some people even came into the salon just to ask, "Is that so-and-so?" Even better, the local TV station did a news story on the picture-perfect promotion.[1]

INTERIOR SPACE

Use your walls to promote your business. If you can afford it, hire a painter (or an art student) to adorn the walls with original murals that relate to your business. Frame awards and newspaper and magazine articles about your company.

TABLES

Place your portfolio on one of your tables, where waiting customers can learn more about your business.

SIGNS

Signage can be one of your most valuable marketing tools, especially if your business has excellent visibility to cars and pedestrians. Make sure your company name is easy to see from a distance, and include fewer than five words to describe your business. Make sure your signage is consistent inside and outside

[1] *Modern Salon,* July 1996, p. 112.

your location. If you have more than one location, be consistent with all signs. Plus, if possible, incorporate a useful item, such as a clock, into your signage, which prompts people to look at it daily during their commute.

VOICE MAIL

Yet another way to make your business seem bigger—and more successful. It is also considered better than answering machines, which can break down while you're retrieving messages. Voice mail is inexpensive and makes you sound like a pro.

THE VOICE ON THE PHONE

Do you have a receptionist? Make sure he or she has a warm, helpful, professional manner. If you can't afford a receptionist, make sure your phone is answered with a straightforward message (no jokes, please) or electronic voice mail. Anything less than this and you won't be taken seriously.

ON-LINE SERVICES

If you don't already have an on-line address, now's the time to get one. Commercial on-line services or Internet service providers open a relatively inexpensive communication channel for your business. Plus, an e-mail address shows your clients and customers that you are technically current, which instills confidence.

YOUR ADDRESS

If yours is strictly a service business, and you can't afford office space in a high-rent district, consider leasing a mailbox in a posh part of town. Your image will be dramatically enhanced. For example, you could rent a box through Mail Boxes Etc. on Wilshire Boulevard, which immediately affords you a Beverly

Hills address—if that's the cachet you seek. Boxes cost about twenty dollars a month and there's a three-month minimum.

LOCATION, LOCATION, LOCATION.

GIVEAWAYS

Offer cappuccino and croissants to customers. Give crayons and coloring books to kids. Little things mean a lot! In Foster, Rhode Island, an Office Plus print shop invites people to make up to five free photocopies every day. "Our walk-in business increased; ten to twenty people come in daily to make free copies," says J. F. Halbrooks, manager. "We get other business from it such as printing, faxing and layout work...it spreads our name around the neighborhood... Surprisingly, some people still leave money for their copies," he adds. "The free copies got people in the door."

2. CREATE GREAT ATMOSPHERE WITH CUSTOMER SERVICE.

Yes, the adage says that new customers are silver while current customers are gold. But you wouldn't have *any* customers without first-class customer service.

Just ask Shirley Fisher, a State Farm insurance agent in Columbia, Missouri, who knows all too well the value of providing extra service and support to customers. Fisher instituted a program geared to new teenage drivers, which has elicited a most enthusiastic response from their parents. Fisher invites new drivers—and their parents—into her office for a twenty-minute talk about driving costs; the effects of tickets and warnings; information on why not to ever loan your car; what to do in case of accidents; and more. This program has proved to be such a hit that parents now call her to schedule an appointment when another child comes of driving age. "It's helped my bottom line and it's made better drivers out of these young people," says Fisher.

PROVIDE ADDITIONAL LONG-TERM VALUE.

In another example, Fisher answered a call from a frantic policy owner whose home was burning down. Fisher spent the entire next day—December 24th—with the family, inspecting the damage. "I was handholding and helping them deal with it," says Fisher. But the results will come back to her tenfold. "It cemented my relationship with them, and they, in turn, will always tell their friends about it," adds Fisher. "People really stay with me because I'm their agent, and because of my service. Just about all of my business comes from referrals."

YOU'VE GOTTA GIVE A LITTLE.

Like Fisher, you should set yourself apart and make an effort to be genuinely interested in your clients. Show them that your concern goes beyond the buck. Mail new and prospective clients useful information such as relevant articles, reports, industry news updates, and invitations to local events that might be of interest. If you're conducting a seminar or workshop, ask them to attend or send them a free ticket. Good, old-fashioned thoughtfulness—and an attitude of giving instead of getting— goes a long way.

Nadine Heaps, owner of an insurance agency in Ashland, Massachusetts, makes it a point to send a small birthday gift to each and every client. It's a friendly reminder that keeps her connected to clients.

Boston pawnbroker Michael Goldstein provides catered homemade breakfast goodies at his store every day from Thanksgiving to Christmas. Goldstein, who has offered this service for the past four years, now gets inquiries beginning in October from hungry customers who ask, "Where's the Danish?"

Another method is to listen and hear what your clients have to say; too few people realize that the art of conversation involves listening, not talking! Prospects are leery of fast-talking business people. Besides, you'll never be able to effectively service your customers if you don't take time to hear their needs.

"NO PROBLEM": TWO WORDS YOUR CUSTOMERS LOVE TO HEAR.

Barry Potekin, owner of Gold Coast Dogs, also knows the great value of service-with-a-smile—and service that goes the extra mile. When he started his Chicago-based restaurant, he realized how bad customer service in this country had become. "Nobody treats nobody good anymore," he laments. "It's a disgrace." So, he taught his employees to live by these credos: "Be genuine. Look the other person in the eye. Be easy to do business with. Little things mean everything."

A big part of their education includes the words "Absolutely" and "No problem," which Potekin sees as "the two greatest words." These are the two answers to practically any question that might be posed at any Gold Coast Dogs restaurant—hypothetical questions such as "May I have mayonnaise on that?" "May I substitute a salad with this order?" or "Can you hold the dressing on that?"

BE POSITIVE.

Hospitality above and beyond can also be found at California Pizza Kitchen, founded in 1985 by two lawyers (and food enthusiasts). All of the employees wear pins that announce their home city, which leads to interesting conversations between wait staff and customers. There's also no charge for soda refills—a small but generous touch that makes a good impression. In addition, kids receive a four-page activity book to keep them busy throughout their meal.

What happens when and if you do care for customer needs—but your business is rejected nonetheless? For one, don't take it personally. Every business has to handle rejections, objections, and postponements, and the way that you handle it can make or break present—and future—sales.

The golden rule is to avoid becoming enemies. Instead of breaking down the client's resistance, work on building agreement. Be patient, listen to the objections, and then "mirror" them back to be sure that you completely understand the problem. When you mirror or paraphrase the other person's points, it shows that you really listened. It's also smart to acknowledge and validate their concerns. Then, show empathy by saying "I understand why you feel that way" and explain why; it will do wonders for breaking down barriers. Develop long-term relationships, even if you're not doing business today.

Dr. Harville Hendrix, in his best-selling books on love and marriage, such as *Getting the Love You Want* (HarperPerennial), calls this technique the "Couples Dialogue," and it can be very effective in making people into allies, not enemies.

Finally, always respond to objections as soon as they are presented; it shows that you have an answer.

3. IMITATE THE "TOP GUNS."

On your way to success, it's wise to follow the examples of top businesses that offer exemplary service that inspires repeat customers. You may not be as big as these companies, but that doesn't mean you can't act like them!

Take Nordstrom, for example. It was founded in 1901 by Carl Wallin, a Seattle shoemaker, and John W. Nordstrom, a Swede who arrived in the United States in 1887 with five dollars in his pocket and little command of the English language. Nordstrom believed that success would come only by offering customers the very best service, selection, quality, and value.

COMMIT TO SERVICING CUSTOMER NEEDS AND DESIRES.

Today, in its tenth decade of operation, that attention to service is legendary. Just note these services that Nordstrom offers to its customers:

- In many stores a concierge provides umbrellas, wheelchairs, and strollers; checks coats, umbrellas, and packages; and provides information about the store. The concierge can also send a fax, issue gift certificates, offer sightseeing suggestions, call cabs, or book restaurant and theater reservations.
- Diaper-changing areas are located in both the men's and women's lounges. In most stores family restrooms are also available so that either parent can take a child to the restroom.
- Shoe shine service is available and is popular with men and women.
- Elegant champagne and silver gift boxes, a long-time customer favorite, are also available in each department of the store, and are complimentary with each purchase.
- And here's one of the most incredible services of all: A few years ago the store in Skokie, Illinois, donated space for a mammography center, housed in a private suite near the cosmetics department and operated by local hospitals. Women may make appointments in advance. Once in the store, they

may stop by the mammography center, and then go shopping; they are paged when it is time for their appointment.

With services like these, why would you even want to shop anywhere else?

OFFER WHAT YOUR COMPETITION HASN'T EVEN THOUGHT OF.

TAKE A RITZY APPROACH

If you've ever stayed at The Ritz-Carlton, you've undoubtedly experienced first-class service. It's all part of The Ritz-Carlton's "Gold Standards" that include a pocket-sized "credo" of twenty principles that all employees must abide by. For example, each employee is to consider himself an ambassador of the hotel, on and off the property. Another point is that each employee must answer the telephone within three rings, and with a "smile." Any employee who receives a customer complaint "owns" it, and has the responsibility to handle it. It also supports a culture of "Ladies and Gentlemen serving Ladies and Gentlemen." Most of all, each employee has the obligation to fulfill "even the unexpressed wishes and needs of our guests."

ANTICIPATE CUSTOMER NEEDS—BEFORE THEY'RE VOICED!

Imagine that. A hotel that tries to anticipate your needs and wants, *before* you even voice them! No wonder then, that, in 1992, The Ritz-Carlton was the first hospitality organization to receive the prestigious Malcolm Baldrige National Quality Award. The award, named after the U.S. Secretary of Commerce during the Reagan administration, was established in 1987 to promote awareness of quality and excellence, to recognize quality achievements of U.S. companies, and to publicize successful quality

strategies. It is awarded each year to small businesses, manu-facturing companies or subsidiaries, and service companies or subsidiaries.

Every smart marketer should follow The Ritz-Carlton's credo. Not sure exactly what your customers need and want? That's where an informal survey comes in handy. Regularly poll your clients to determine how you could better your service; it may be just the thing to propel you ahead of the competition.

Whether or not you want to believe it, perception is every-thing, and customers make decisions based on their perception of your business. Make sure that you create a great impression in person, on paper, and in your surroundings. Not only will you feel good about it, but it will attract your customers.

Now that you look as good on paper as you do in person, it's time to venture onward—and outward. Now's the time to form strategic alliances with people who can help your business, which we will discuss in Chapter 4.

PART ONE RESOURCES:

COMPANY AND PRODUCT NAMING
NameStar
19 Westgate, Suite 4
Chestnut Hill, MA 02467
(617) 325-0797

LOGOS
Jeff Fisher LogoMotives
P.O. Box 6631
Portland, OR 97228-6631
(503) 283-8673
Fax: (503) 283-8995
www.jfisherlogomotives.com
Primarily works with small businesses and entrepreneurs to create identities.

The Logo Works, Inc.
P.O. Box 1472
Davidson, NC 28036
(704) 576-6100
www.thelogoworksinc.com
Specializes in creating affordable, quality logos for new businesses.

PHOTO REPRODUCTION HOUSES
ABC Pictures
1867 East Florida St.
Springfield, MO 65803
(888)526-5336
Produces high-quality lithographic prints, which cost less than standard photographs. These are great to include in press kits and packages, although they are not suitable for reprinting in newspapers.

Mass Photo Co.
1315 Waugh Dr.
Houston, TX 77019
(800) 306-7883
Mass-produced photos made from your original photo, artwork, negative, or transparency. Great for sales promotions, new product introductions, headshots, etc.

NRS Photos
681 North Perkins
Appleton, WI 54914
(800) 972-8108
Produces high-quality lithographic prints plus duplications of genuine gloss photographs, which are suitable for newspaper reproduction.

WRITERS
American Society of Journalists and Authors, Inc.
Dial-A-Writer
150 Broadway, Suite 302
New York, NY 10036
(212) 398-1934
Fax: (212) 768-7414

National Writers Union
National Office
(with 13 local chapters)
113 University Place, 6th floor
New York, NY 10003
(212) 254-0279

PEOPLE WHO NEED PEOPLE

FouR

GIVE-AND-TAKE WITH A BOARD OF ADVISORS

> **No man is an island, entire of itself; every man is a piece of the continent, a part of the main. . . . Any man's death diminishes me because I am involved in mankind, and therefore never send to know for whom the bell tolls; it tolls for thee.**
>
> JOHN DONNE, *DEVOTIONS UPON EMERGENT OCCASIONS, MEDITATION XVII*, 1624

1. Don't go it alone.
2. Persist—but don't be pushy.
3. Select professionals who complement your business.

John Donne was right. No man is an island. To succeed in business, you need to work with and rely on others, because it's almost impossible to do everything alone.

Barbra Streisand was also correct when she sang, "People who need people are the luckiest people in the world."

1. DON'T GO IT ALONE.

Interdependence may seem contrary to the entrepreneurial spirit, especially in our culture. We have built an entire mythology around the notion of the pioneering adventurer, cutting swaths in the corporate jungle without benefit of organization or association. But the reality is, nobody truly makes it alone.

Successful entrepreneurs are adept at forming alliances and are proficient at leveraging these to further their career goals. They understand that a business is built on people, plural. By establishing mutually beneficial transactions with others, you will not only boost your business, you will gain a considerable bonus: personal relationships.

Consider how important others are to us in our personal lives. We depend on family and friends to listen to our ideas, to serve as sounding boards, to help us work through problems, to supplement our own skills and talents, and to ease our work load. We have these same needs in our professional lives, especially as small business owners who don't have a vast in-office support system. Interdependence puts us in touch with those who can fulfill these needs. The lone explorer, on the other hand, is likely to get lost in the wilderness.

You need customers as well as professionals upon whom you can rely for advice. And it all starts with a Board of Advisors.

2. PERSIST—BUT DON'T BE PUSHY.

Doug Mellinger, chairman and CEO of PRT Group Inc., which is headquartered in New York City, didn't start out with a Board of Advisors, because "I didn't know what a Board of Advisors was. I needed mentors." So Mellinger brought together a group of chief information officers, "who were the ultimate buyers," says Mellinger. (PRT Group is a global software engineering services company that works with clients to increase the business value of technology by aligning application strategies with business objectives.) Mellinger simply got on the phone and called the chairman of Pepsi, who introduced him to Pepsi's CIO.

Then Mellinger pored over an issue of *CIO Magazine*, a trade journal for the Fortune 500. He put together a list of candidates whom he would call at 7:30 A.M.—"before the secretaries were there." The first person he called was "the Number One guy at

Merrill Lynch. I kept calling him until he'd see me. It took months until I got an appointment."

When Mellinger met with him, he simply asked him if he'd be his mentor. "I asked him if he'd see me every six to eight weeks so I could ask his advice on what I would do, and get feedback," says Mellinger. "He said 'Sure.' He didn't know what he was getting into!"

Mellinger's Board of Advisors has never been paid. "Some thought it was fun. They'd say that watching me grow was like watching their son grow," Mellinger adds.

"I advise everybody to do it," says Mellinger. "Go right to the top... Most of them (corporate executives) don't get asked. People are afraid to ask and it blows me away."

One of the greatest advantages of his Board of Advisors, Mellinger adds, is that "they've really beaten us up to stay on a straight path. They reel me in...in the early days I thought I was invincible...they reminded me I didn't have enough resources and they were my safety net and protected me from myself."

Today, PRT has approximately nine hundred employees and eleven locations worldwide.

If you had a huge disposable income, you could hire a public-relations firm and pay them to market and promote your business. But here's the next-best thing: you can set up a Board of Advisors; these folks will become your publicist as well as your sounding board, consultant, and resource for referrals. The cost to you? Some time and effort, as well as the price of light refreshments and parking expenses.

What exactly is a Board of Advisors? It is a mentoring group composed of colleagues, respected community members, fellow entrepreneurs, and anyone who can assist with the development and growth of your new business. Yes, your advisors advise, but they do not have voting shares in your company, as does a Board of Directors.

3. SELECT PROFESSIONALS WHO COMPLEMENT YOUR BUSINESS.

Ideally, you should have a professional or friendly relationship with your board members. Seek a diverse group, which will offer the utmost in balance and perspective; each member should bring a different skill to the table, so choose wisely from professionals in fields that complement your business and each other. You won't need five lawyers on your board; instead, you may seek a lawyer plus a certified public accountant, marketing consultant, writer, computer consultant, sales executive, even a local physician or dentist. If you sell to people within specific industries—if you have a specific niche market—it's wise to include a representative from your prospect base who can also bring his or her expertise to the table. Although you may want to pay your Board of Advisors, it's not necessary. However, it may make people more accountable if they are to attend meetings and provide you with ongoing advice. Just remember to be as specific as possible in your requests.

How do you get others to help you? For one, you must project a professional, consistent image, showing everyone that you mean business and are also accountable to them. Approach each prospective board member with a phone call, then follow up with a letter spelling out your request (see the example on p. 50). Establish reasonable goals and time commitments, such as quarterly Thursday breakfast meetings of no more than one hour.

ASK FOR THE HELP YOU NEED.

What, besides the possibility of payment, do your advisors get out of helping you? They can enjoy the advantage of a tremendous networking opportunity with other board members, thanks to your business. They also know that you're likely to return the favor by assisting them in the future. Make sure to offer before they even have to ask.

WHAT'S IN IT FOR THEM?

After your board is assembled, determine the most convenient meeting time and location for each member, then strike a compromise. Before each meeting, send each member a copy of the agenda (see p. 51); it should include introductions, the current status of your business, its future considerations, customer or client development, information about your industry, future projects or plans, and a review of commitments for the next meeting. After each meeting, send each participant a copy of the meeting minutes.

FOLLOW THESE LOGISTICS

Your board members should also receive a listing of each participant, plus their addresses and phone numbers.

Likewise, you should offer your services to other professionals who need a Board of Advisors. You already know that it's a savvy way to promote your business.

BE READY, WILLING, AND ABLE TO RETURN THE FAVOR.

Besides offering excellent advice, a Board of Advisors will, almost always, lead you to referrals, thus creating possibilities for even more business.

TWO AND MORE HEADS ARE BETTER THAN ONE

Just ask Ann Higgins. She is president and owner of Danlee/DHM Group in Red Bank New Jersey; her firm specializes in public relations for high-end consumer products, such as wine and spirits, prestige watches, and lingerie.

When Higgins started her business in 1995, it was just her and one employee. The third week into business they started "Creative Cooperatives," a group similar to a Board of Advisors, "because I was asked to present something and I panicked," says Higgins. "We felt when it was just two of us, we had certain limitations. We tended to see things in a certain way. We didn't want to get stale."

So Higgins invited friends and acquaintances with small businesses to get together for periodic brainstorming sessions. She promised to keep the sessions to a maximum hour and a half, and also offered lunch. "I would give them an incentive to loan us their brain," Higgins says.

Before each meeting, she would send them a briefing page with the topic to be discussed. "Then we would sit and have a creative brainstorming session," she adds.

She credits Creative Cooperatives with helping to double her business in the first year. The first group of people came from different disciplines: new news media, a production company, and public relations, but with a different focus. She found that each brought a different perspective. "The video production person had a very visual streak. The new media person had different ways to reach people."

Often, the makeup of the group varies depending on the issue they're discussing. Once, when they had a new product that was targeted to males twenty-five to thirty-five years old, Higgins had a junior account executive round up some friends for a creative session.

The groups tend to have five or six people, though there can be as many as ten. "If you do more, you lose control of the creative session," Higgins says. "You have too many opinions, and you're bound to go over the allotted ninety minutes."

She found that all the people she calls on are happy to help. "What I found was that because everyone was struggling with the same issues as business owners, they were glad to help." Now it's evolved into a support network. Members are a source of information and encouragement to one another. They frequently telephone one another for advice.

Higgins is active with the American Business Women's Association and the National Association of Women Business Owners, and tends to solicit members for Creative Cooperatives through these and other networking organizations. Her philosophy is that small business people need one another. "You need to build a support network to be successful. If you don't have it, you're in trouble.

"The flip side to that is you have to be very helpful (to others)," she adds.

Yet another way to successfully market your small business is by word-of-mouth referrals. That's what the next chapter is all about.

Five

SEEK
WORD-OF-MOUTH
REFERRALS

**Why is it that I get my best ideas in the
morning when I'm shaving?**
ALBERT EINSTEIN

1. Cross-promote when possible.
2. Join or start an association.
3. Barter and network.

Another of the "interdependent" marketing tools is to market your business through word-of-mouth referrals. When you're launching a business, your satisfied customers can be your biggest and most cost-effective and credible asset, as they'll do all of the talking! That third-party endorsement is worth its weight in marketing gold, and it won't cost anything either.

Beth Evans attributes much of the success of her Nailtiques nail-care products to word-of-mouth marketing. She launched her products in Great Neck, New York, and also in Florida, where her Great Neck clients frequently traveled. She made presentations at salons and beauty stores, and left behind numerous free samples and literature. Evans eventually got the products into Bloomingdale's. "After that the phone didn't stop ringing," says Evans. "The product took off....We did no advertising. It was all word-of-mouth."

Word-of-mouth is an advantage because you get other people to do the marketing for you. Network marketing companies like Nikken and Amway, have all thrived because they relied on word-of-mouth advertising.

Being good at what you do, or having an interesting business, creates conversation about you among clients and prospects.

1. CROSS-PROMOTE WHEN POSSIBLE.
Blockbuster Video and Pizza Hut do it... So why can't you?

Another smart marketing technique is to work with other local businesses, doing cross-promotions. For example, a make-up artist who wants to book more bridal clients might hook up with a hotel that wants to do more wedding business. The make-up artist would promote the hotel's wedding package to her clients—by keeping its wedding package information handy—while the hotel would market her beauty services in its package to brides; each company would offer special discounts to brides who utilize both businesses. In addition, the two businesses can split the costs of signage and promotion. Faster than you can say, "I Do," you've got an ideal marriage of two businesses!

For example, we know of a writer who cross-promotes her services with a printer. She recommends the printer to her clients in need of professional materials; in turn, the printer recommends her for editing and proofreading.

- Wedding videographers could cross-promote with print photographers and film/camera stores.
- A video rental store could cross-promote with a take-out food delivery service or candy store.
- A massage therapist could cross-promote with a health-food store, nutrition consultant, or chiropractor.

As Zig Ziglar, the guru of sales once said, "The more you help others get what they want, the more you get of what you want."

2. JOIN OR START AN ASSOCIATION.

Does your business belong to a professional association? This is yet another way to take advantage of shared resources, and networking possibilities. Many associations also offer products onto which you can emblazon your business name, and turn into a free giveaway. For example, acupuncturists can get informational brochures from the American Academy of Medical Acupuncture in Los Angeles, and simply add their name and address on the front. *Gale's Encyclopedia of Associations* is a great resource for this information.

If your industry doesn't have an association, start your own association. You'll be able to pool your resources—and your knowledge—to help your business and others in your industry! That's what Paula Coy and Paula Delaney did. The co-owners of Pet-ercise, a pet-sitting service in Westwood, Massachusetts, found that their pet-sitting services weren't taken seriously. So in 1993 they formed the New England Association of Pet-Sitters, which today has thirty-five members across eastern Massachusetts. The association, says Delaney, improved the bottom line and also adds credibility. "Our business is taken more seriously now," she says. In addition, the association generates press coverage, allows all members to pool their resources to purchase newspaper advertising and booths at pet expos and dog shows, and to finance mass mailings to veterinarians, dog groomers, and Humane Societies.

3. BARTER AND NETWORK.

Yet another way to get word-of-mouth referrals, and improve the bottom line, is through bartering.

"Small businesses rely heavily on us," says Ray Bastarache, owner of Barter Network in Milford, Connecticut, a clearing-house for more than three thousand New England businesses that include printers, radio stations, dentists, shoe repair shops, and jewelry stores. The advantage to small businesses? "Number one—they get increased sales," says Bastarache. "Bartering brings you incremental business over and beyond your business."

The second advantage is that bartering increases your cash flow. "It's better to barter than to write a check," Bastarache continues. "There's also a lot of cash business that gets generated," he adds. "Let's say you use an attorney that you like—then you'll tell your friends," Bastarache says. "The spinoff business is very beneficial."

Third, bartering moves excess inventory. "Let's say you have one hundred thousand dollars in excess inventory in your warehouse," Bastarache says. "You can sell it for cash and liquidate it for much less than it's worth or you can get the full value of it by converting it into bartered goods and services...or getting advertising to attract a cash business for the product," he adds.

In addition, bartering "uplifts people's lifestyles," says Bastarache. "It lets you have things you usually can't afford," he says.

However, bartering isn't for everyone. "If you're swamped with cash business, bartering is not your mechanism," Bastarache cautions. "Bartering really works for companies with products and professionals with excess time."

Remember, it's not enough to simply join an association, or industry organization, and attend monthly meetings. You also need to sign up for a committee where you can make an impact and also meet potential clients and gain new referrals. Another smart idea is to join professional organizations outside of your industry, because that's where you're most likely to meet people who will want and need your services. For example, a caterer may meet more corporate event-planners by joining the local Chamber of Commerce rather than the caterer's association. In fact, many professional organizations often sponsor functions during nonbusiness hours, specifically for networking purposes.

After you master the meeting-and-greeting of networking, follow up with your new contacts. There's an advertising rule of thumb that says that consumers need exposure to a product six or seven times before they connect it with its ad. As entrepreneurs, you need to adopt the same strategies.

Networking is also a tried-and-true way to drum up business. To be effective, however, don't just make small talk while you're eating those hors d'oeuvres. Make it your goal to meet up to five new people, and make notes about them on the back of their business cards. Ask them questions about their business, and make sure that you can sum up yours succinctly in one sentence.

Where to network? Check out professional organizations in and out of your field, as well as business groups such as the Chamber of Commerce. Even annual holiday parties can provide an opportunity. And don't overlook bumping into a business associate or potential customers at the bank or supermarket. When you work for yourself, you should always be ready to network—regardless of where you are! (See p. 51 for more networking ideas.)

As you become known within your industry, and among your clients and their industries, you're actually laying a solid foundation for taking your reputation to the next level. You can do that by further establishing your expertise and credibility. That's what the next chapter is all about—writing, speaking, and creating opportunities to see and be seen.

SAMPLE LETTER FOR BOARD OF ADVISORS

Date

Name
Title
Company
Address

Dear _____:

It was a pleasure to speak with you this week regarding my request for you to be on my Board of Advisors. As we discussed, my business is undergoing many positive changes and your advice and expertise in sales and marketing [or other] is just what I need at this important time.

I realize how busy you are and appreciate your willingness to commit to meetings with me and other board members to discuss the development of my business. Your assistance and solid advice has been an enormous help to me in the past, and I know it will be in the future as well.

Our meetings will be held on a quarterly basis at the Boston Center for Adult Education beginning on Tuesday, April 4. We will meet from 8:00 to 9:30 A.M. and a continental breakfast will be served. I will prepare a meeting agenda and send it to you the week prior to our meeting. After each meeting, I will send you the minutes, plus an outline of my action steps for the next few months.

_____, I will call you to confirm your attendance at the April 4th meeting, and I have enclosed directions and parking instructions for your convenience. Thank you again for your continued support of me and my business. Please know that I am available to assist you in any way possible. If you have any questions, please call me at (xxx) xxx-xxxx.

Warm regards,

_____

Enclosures

SAMPLE AGENDA OF BOARD OF ADVISORS MEETING (ON LETTERHEAD)

Board of Advisors Meeting
Date

- Introductions
  List of Board Members with addresses and phone numbers
- Your business
  Description of its current situation and future considerations
- Client development
- Product development
  Book
  Workbook
  Audiotape series
- Trade show participation
  Booth display
  Pre- and post-show marketing
  Seminar
  Key contacts to meet
- Future projects
- Review commitments for the next meeting

PART TWO RESOURCES:

Accelerated Networking
Audiotape from Net-Works Sales Tools
$12, 40 minutes
(800) 371-2264
51 Spenser Brook Rd.
Carlisle, MA 01701
By Nancy Stephens

Networking Smart: How to Build Relationships for Personal and Organizational Success
By Wayne E. Baker

Networking for Success
Learning video from Net-Works
  Sales Tools
$49.99, 25 minutes
(800) 371-2264
51 Spenser Brook Rd.
Carlisle, MA 01701
By Nancy Stephens

THE POWER OF PRESTIGE AND EXPERTISE

Six

DO THE WRITE THING

1. Make it snap, crackle, and pop!
2. Publish or perish.
3. Tell—don't sell.

In 1979 many DJs emceed college events and weddings with homemade equipment and records borrowed from friends. Randy Barth decided to change all that; he founded Rack-A-Disc (now known as Premier Talent Group), a professional disc jockey company with strict guidelines and state-of-the-art equipment. Barth also wanted to set his business apart by making himself into an expert on wedding music and DJs. So, in addition to buying ad space in a local, start-up bridal magazine, Barth offered to write free articles in which he would share his DJ expertise with brides, and educate them about hiring a DJ for their wedding. It worked. "We got more calls from the articles than the ads," says Barth. "It added clout. People need to see your name in print. The goal is to have people wanting you, instead of you wanting them. Then they come searching for you."

Barth did one of the smartest things a small business person can do. He parlayed his expertise into a magazine column, thus increasing his visibility and credibility as an authority on wedding planning. And let's face it—opportunities frequently arise when other people read your advice. Of course they also come knocking when others can hear you, or see you; just ask any actor who has been "discovered."

When you make yourself—and your business—visible, it not only sets you apart from the competition, it also establishes you as a credible, reliable source of information about your field. It takes your expertise and puts it into the forefront, where it's apt to get noticed. Not only does visibility impress others and lift your status; it also can lead to increased consumer confidence and a healthier bottom line.

VISIBILITY = CREDIBILITY = NAME RECOGNITION.

Remember—experts are always in demand. And there are two tried-and-true ways to make yourself into an expert—writing and public speaking.

1. MAKE IT SNAP, CRACKLE, AND POP!

There's no doubt that writing articles can give you an edge. It not only establishes you as an expert in your field, it also publicizes your company, reinforces your image, enhances your credibility, and adds instant prestige.

Writing might not guarantee you fame and fortune; then again, it just might. Just make sure to implement the "Rice Krispies" rule of writing,

The Advantages of Writing

- Reinforces your company image
- Establishes you as an expert in your field
- Cost-effectively publicizes your company
- Enhances your credibility
- Offers prestige

which means that your words should snap, crackle, pop—and leap—off the page!

2. PUBLISH OR PERISH.

First things first: Author an article with your "byline" or a tag line—your name, a short description of your company, and phone number—and get your name in print. Writing for your local newspaper or trade publication can work wonders for your business and help make your audience more familiar and comfortable with your product or service. When your article appears in print, you are essentially speaking directly to thousands of potential customers and clients.

Every article should contain your name, company name, a brief description of your business, city and state where you're located, and any other impressive things worth mentioning—perhaps you've also authored a workbook, an audiotape, or regularly write for a trade journal.

MAKE SURE READERS CAN EASILY CONTACT YOU.

Where to publish your prose? Trade and alumni publications, local newspapers, newsletters, and nonprofit publications all have space that needs to be filled. In addition, check out professional organizations that you belong to, and ascertain if they have any authorship needs. If they don't pay, volunteer to do it. The results can be enormous. However, bear in mind that the payoff might not be monetary, and financial reward might not come for years. But the visibility and credibility gained are usually worth it.

ME, WRITE?

Here's a breakdown of the advantages and disadvantages of some writing markets.

EXTERNAL WRITING MARKETS

LOCAL NEWSPAPER
Pros: Easy to break into. Can lead to wider coverage.
Cons: Limited audience. Small payment, if any.

NATIONAL NEWSPAPER
Pros: Excellent exposure nationally. Good payment rates. Prestige.
Cons: Hard to break into. Former writing experience and samples usually required.

BUSINESS JOURNALS
Pros: Excellent exposure to business types; can lead to a wealth of opportunities.
Cons: Difficult to break into.

INTERNAL WRITING MARKETS

TRADE JOURNALS
Pros: Speaking directly to your industry and target market. Exposing your expertise to your peers and colleagues. Networking possibilities because of common industry.
Cons: Limited audience.

ALUMNI MAGAZINE
Pros: Diverse audience. Networking possibilities because of common interests.
Cons: Limited audience who may not even be your customers.

NEWSLETTERS
Pros: Targeting your ideal markets. Becoming known within various industries.
Cons: Limited exposure. Small payment, if any.

BRAINSTORM AND BEGIN!

After targeting the publications you'd like to write for, brainstorm and list all of the possible articles you might write for various sections of the periodical. Here are some suggestions.

- Op-eds: opinion pieces submitted to editorial pages or the "My Turn" section of *Newsweek;* letters to the editor.
- Columns: regular specialized features such as those written by Ellen Goodman and William Safire. "Ask the expert" columns like those by Heloise and Ann Landers. (A description of your business goes at the end.)
- Feature stories: "how-to" or news stories for the Food, Arts, Living, or Home sections.
- Business trends: articles about new trends in your industry.
- First-person articles: advice-packed pieces loaded with solid information you've gleaned from your business experience. Sometimes you can even make these humorous.

3. TELL—DON'T SELL.

To have value, your articles must be informative and not mere advertisements. Ask each publication for its lead time—most magazines work three to four months in advance—and for a current editorial calendar, to see if there are any topics you could plug your story into. (Newspapers, obviously, have a shorter lead time than magazines.) You should also ask for writer's guidelines to find out how long articles should be and how they should be submitted; nowadays, most publications ask for double-spaced hard copy plus a computer disk, or a submission via e-mail. Most important, propose your idea in the form of a query letter. (More on query letters follows.)

OFFER VALUABLE INFORMATION TO THE READER.

What if you can't write, or you simply don't have the time? That's when it's handy to hire a ghostwriter—someone who will write for you without taking credit; you use his (or her) words but put your name on the manuscript. You can post a writing job with the National Writers Union and the American Society of Journalists and Authors. You should also contact local reporters and teachers of writing classes at your community college or adult education center, and ask if they do any freelance work. College alumni offices may also post a job for alums looking for part-time work. This way, you can give them your raw data and information, and then they work their magic on their computers.

HIRE A GOOD WRITER!

HOW TO GET PUBLISHED

Getting published isn't as difficult or as intimidating as you might think. The first step is to research your market. What magazines, for example, would you like to write for? After drawing up a list, there are several things you can do. First, call the magazine's advertising department and request a media kit and rate card. This will give you an idea of the magazine's departments and reader demographics. Call the editorial department and also request an editorial calendar for the next six months, plus their writer's guidelines outlining the type of articles they're looking for. Then, go to the library and read all the issues from the last six months to a year. This will give you a good idea of the articles they've already done, so you won't waste their time with a repetitive idea. All of this information will help you pitch a story that's interesting, unique, and different. It may also help you to discover a need that the periodical isn't filling. Propose your ideas to the publication, and include sample articles, if you have any.

Sometimes you can simply call an editor and just ask about the kinds of stories he or she is looking for. We've done it ourselves, and it never ceases to amaze us how much information an editor—with a few moments to spare—is willing to divulge.

Some magazines ask that you submit a query letter. A query letter is just that—a letter that proposes the story you wish to write, and the reason you are the ideal person to write it. Point out your expertise, your unique qualifications, and the angle that you wish to pursue. Make sure that you start your letter with a sentence that will capture the editor's attention. (For more information, read *How to Write Irresistible Query Letters* by Lisa Collier Cool.) Two sample query letters are given on pages 66 and 68.

WRITE TO BE READ

Just as you've made your query letter interesting and dynamic, do the same with your actual article. Make your story informative, interesting, provocative, humorous—whatever—so that the words leap off of the page and have readers clamoring for the next sentence.

Informative—Include information that will be helpful to the reader. For example, travel stories frequently include where to stay, where to dine, shopping tips, best beaches, and other useful data.

Provocative—Two words: Howard Stern.

Humorous—The popularity of Spam in Hawaii is an offbeat, unusual story, and not the typical feature usually written about the Aloha State. Or, perhaps you recently hosted a booth at a trade show, and couldn't believe (a) how tired you became, (b) the mountains of freebies that were given away, and (c) how many times you said "Hello." You could work this material into a funny first-person account of your experiences for an industry trade journal.

Controversial—One word: Madonna.

Here's another example. Sometimes companies get worldwide attention because they create controversy—and positive PR—where there previously was none. For example, in 1987, Allen-Edmonds Shoe Company CEO John Stollenwerk was disheartened on his return from a business trip, to find that his company had been denied its application to display its footwear at the Tokyo Shoe Fair. When he discovered that the Europeans had been invited, he got mad. So he packed up his shoes and took the next flight to Tokyo—but only after he called the media and exclaimed, "I'm not the ugly American, I'm the *angry* American." Even before he boarded his flight, he was bombarded by media attention—and the Japanese wound up letting him show his shoes. To this day, Stollenwerk is remembered as the gutsy man who crashed the Japanese shoe show.

Slice of Life—What may not have inherent news value may find itself on the features pages as a slice-of-life story, in *Newsweek*'s "My Turn" column or the "His point of view" section of a woman's magazine. Karpowicz, for example, has written first-person, humorous magazine articles about her various experiences, including how she stayed thin on a cruise ship (for *Weight Watchers*); a feature about a day-in-the-life of a model for a boudoir photographer (for a bridal magazine); and a Living section newspaper story about her take on a new type of facial.

WRITE ON!

After you've written an article, don't stop there. Make sure to use it in all your marketing efforts. Make photocopies on high-quality paper stock or buy reprints, to mail to prospects, clients, and media contacts—and to include in your portfolio and promotional kit. It's a smart way for others to get up-close-and-personal with your business, and they'll probably be impressed with your expertise. If you cut-and-paste the article to make photocopies, lay it out so everything fits attractively on one page, with the masthead and date at the top.

Always have copies on hand to use as handouts and giveaways at your speaking engagements. If you can, publish all or some of your article in your own newsletter, or in a client newsletter (with permission from the periodical).

SHOW OFF YOUR ARTICLES.

POSITION YOURSELF BY WRITING BOOKS AND MORE

Want to follow in the well heeled footsteps of Susan Powter or Tony Robbins? The answer lies in getting published as a book author. Chances are, you have your own unique expertise—even if there are other "experts" offering advice on the same subject. Being a published author not only crystallizes your expertise, but also adds to your prestige and offers you the chance at a marketing gold mine. Who knows? The right book could put you on next year's "What's Hot" list! (See pp.106 and 107 for a listing of publishing resources.)

There are four basic routes in publishing: books, self-published books, booklets, and newsletters.

BOOKS

Pros: Great money-making potential; can lead to a wealth of other opportunities—talk shows, seminars, book tours, second and third books—all of which underscore your position as an expert.

Cons: Time-consuming to write, research, and pitch to editors—while still working full time.

SELF-PUBLISHED BOOKS

Pros: Same advantages as with books, but you must understand the hows and whys of distribution.

Cons: Time-consuming to write, research, and market—all on your own. May require an editorial assistant or publicist, which can be costly.

BOOKLETS

Pros: Can be written quickly. Can be sponsored by associations or organizations, and sold in bulk.

Cons: Doesn't offer the credibility or visibility of a book. Has to be self-published.

NEWSLETTERS

Pros: Can be self-serving. Excellent target marketing to new and potential clients. Great venue for pitching products and services. Sent on a regular basis, they can keep your name in front of customers—and the media.

Cons: Can be expensive to produce and time-consuming.

BY HOOK OR CROOK...WRITE A BOOK!

If you find it easy to write and pitch your expertise, consider writing a book. That's exactly what Carole Jackson did when she wrote *Color Me Beautiful,* the book that showed women everywhere what colors worked best for them, based on the colors of their eyes, skin, and hair. It all happened after Jackson did a formal study of color and its application to clothing, makeup, and hair. Then she taught classes to show women how to put themselves together, using her color techniques. Eventually Jackson's classes formed the basis for her book.[1]

It's also what Jacqueline Smith did. The former owner of a bridal shop in Guild, New Hampshire, Smith strove to make her store stand out from the competition. After years of compiling bridal tips and information, Smith's book, *The Creative Wedding Idea Book,* was published in 1994, after months of searching for an agent and publisher, and writing and rewriting. It paid off; customers browsing in the store would see the book on display and usually make a purchase. "Brides would buy a dress because of the book," Smith says. Later, the *Boston Globe* did a full-page story on Smith, and AT&T invited her to write an article for a business booklet on how to publicize your business.

AUTHORSHIP = EXPERTISE.

If you can't produce an agent, self-publish your own book. Greg Godek, a romance expert, did just that. Why? "Because I

---

[1] *Color Me Beautiful,* Acropolis Books, 1980, p. 10.

was in a hurry; it would have taken a year to eighteen months with a publisher," says Godek, author of numerous books including *1001 Ways to be Romantic*. "I wanted to control it," Godek adds. "You simply find a distribution company and let them do the rest. The advantage is that you have control of the entire product and the entire timeline. The disadvantage is that you pay for everything." To ensure his success, Godek made sure he had a good title and solid content, then exhibited at the American Bookseller's Association convention. "I also give lots of books away—maybe five thousand a year," he adds. "I turned a profit in one and a half years, but I am in the great minority."

Does writing a book seem like too much hard work? Then create your own newsletter in which you offer good information to your clients and associates. Include a strong feature story, reading list, information about new and existing clients, new product introductions, and news about existing accounts and recent accomplishments. Write a personal greeting to your readers and include your photo for maximum visibility. Publish your newsletter on a regular basis, using the same colors as your stationery and collateral materials. You may want to hire ghostwriters, and even ask members of your staff to write articles so they can see their byline in print.

After you have a few bylined articles under your belt, you can leverage your exposure with speaking engagements—the subject of Chapter 7.

SAMPLE QUERY LETTER 1

Date

Lisa Thomas
Associate Business Editor
Home Office Computing
411 Lafayette St.
New York, NY 10003

Dear Lisa:

It was a pleasure to speak with you today regarding the possibility of my writing articles on marketing your business for *Home Office Computing*.

I have enclosed information on my company, Impression Impact, for your review; I've also enclosed bylined articles that I have written for the *Canton Citizen* and the *New England Real Estate Journal*. Recently, I have signed on as a regular contributor to the *Middlesex News* with a bimonthly column, "Market Ability." In addition, I am a regular columnist for other small business publications such as *BJ's Journal* and write a syndicated column for Scripps-Howard.

In addition, I host a weekly radio program, *Making It in Business*, on WADN radio in Concord, Massachusetts, and host a cable-television program, *In the Business*. I recently interviewed Jim Koch, president of The Boston Beer Company, and maker of Samuel Adams beer; George Naddaff and Louis Kane, co-chairmen of Au Bon Pain, for my television and radio programs. I'm also writing a book on marketing tips and recently signed with the Jeff Herman Literary Agency in New York.

I wish to propose these story ideas.

- Becoming the Star in Your Marketing Efforts.

How have business owners used their "celebrity" appeal to increase sales of their business? From Frank Perdue to Dave Thomas, more and more entrepreneurs are using themselves in their advertising and publicity to promote their products and services. Interviews with rising stars on the horizon will be included in this marketing feature.

I will also provide examples of each of these marketing techniques.

- Media Madness—How to Generate Media Interest in You and Your Business.

The process of building relationships with the media is not as difficult as you might expect. Aligning yourself as a resource to a reporter, rather than working constantly to "pitch" them a story about your latest service or invention, will score your company bigger points in the long run. Suggestions from business owners as well as the media will be included.

- No- and Low-Cost Ways to Promote Your Business.

You needn't spend a bundle to put your best foot forward. I can show you how to:

- Create a consistent corporate identity
- Build lasting and mutually beneficial relationships
- Increase your visibility among prospects and clients
- Provide exceptional customer service

Lisa, have a wonderful holiday. I will call you next week to arrange a mutually convenient time for us to speak when I visit New York City. Please call me if you have any questions; I can be reached at [phone number].

Best regards,

Nancy Michaels

SAMPLE QUERY LETTER 2

Date

Tim Lyster
Editor
Continental magazine (in-flight)
Cadmus Custom Publishing
101 Huntington Ave.
Boston, MA 02199

Dear Tim:

Hawaii. It's the land of refreshing piña coladas. Award-winning regional cuisine. Chocolate macadamia nuts. And Spam. Spam?

Yes, believe it or not, Hawaii leads the world in Spam consumption, where, since World War II, it has been the perfect complement to the short-grain sticky rice that everyone eats. It's so popular, in fact, that last year the upscale department store Liberty House even held a Spamboree.

I would like to write a humorous article on this offbeat subject for *Continental magazine*. I have already interviewed the public-relations people at Hormel; a gourmet-store owner in Oahu; a Kauai resident who keeps it in his car; and the lucky Hawaiian woman who won the Spam recipe contest for her "Spicy Eggplant with Spam." (Her prize? A trip to Hormel's factory during its July Spam festival.) At the Spamboree she even wore her favorite earrings—mini replicas of Spam cans. (They're just $12.50 in the "Spamtastic" catalog.)

In addition, I also interviewed a Hawaiian stand-up comic, Frank de Lima, who graciously sent me the lyrics to a song he wrote on Spam, sung to the music of The Village People's "YMCA." ("Tasty, give me meat from a vat; Yes it's tasty, molded square and sliced flat; Yes it's tasty, 63 percent fat".... You get the idea.) I wish to incorporate this information into a sidebar.

I am a full-time journalist and former editor of *The Robb Report*. My travel, lifestyle and business articles have appeared in numerous publications including *Cigar Aficionado, First for Women, Endless Vacation, Trump's, Weight Watchers*, and *Bridal Guide*. Currently I am also a regular contributor to the *Boston Herald* on a wealth of subjects. My forte—and my favorite method—is writing humorous articles on offbeat subjects; please see the cruise story on SITMAR ("Sex Is Too Much After Ravioli"), which I have enclosed.

Tim, I have enclosed my bio and many samples of my published writing. I will call you in a week or two to follow up.

In the meantime, if you want some super Spam recipes to impress your friends, just give me a call. Thank you for your consideration.

Cordially, (or Indigestibly yours,)

Debbi J. Karpowicz

Note: Although this is a freelance writer's query letter, it could also apply to small companies in the travel or food industry, or really anyone who is a Spam aficionado. Although not a hard-hitting business story, an offbeat, even humorous article can still show your expertise and be equally valuable. Just make sure to add your name and business at the end of the story.

SeVEn

SEEK OUT AND SPEAK OUT

All the great speakers were bad speakers at first.
RALPH WALDO EMERSON

1. Practice makes perfect.
2. Speak to your audience.
3. Maximize every speaking engagement.

Public speaking, like writing, also reinforces your company image, establishes you as an expert in your field, and cost effectively advertises your company. And it doesn't take a rocket scientist to realize that those things are great for profits! In addition, public speaking, by forcing you to perform in front of an audience, can also increase your self-esteem—and who couldn't use a little more of that?

"Yikes!" you're saying now. "How can I possibly compete with Lee Iacocca, or Miss Piggy, for that matter?

The Advantages of Public Speaking:

- Increases your self-confidence
- Offers great visibility and exposure
- Cost-effective way to achieve credibility
- Makes you into an expert

We realize, dear reader, that public speaking shares much in common with air travel and dental appointments. The mere thought is dreadful to countless people. In fact, speaking before an audience ranks among the top fears of most Americans.

However, overcoming those anxieties and becoming a proficient public speaker can do wonders for your business—before, during, and after the speech. Remember, every time you deal with a customer, you are honing your public-speaking skills. You're simply doing it in front of one person—not thousands!

There are many organizations that can help you improve your speaking style and learn to deal with the madding crowds, including the National Speakers Association and Toastmasters International, which offers practice and solid information on developing your oratory skills. Since 1924 more than 3 million men and women have benefited from Toastmasters, the world's largest organization devoted to the improvement of public speaking, communication, and leadership skills. There are more than eight thousand clubs throughout the States. There's a sixteen-dollar initiation fee plus annual dues of thirty-six dollars. (See p. 105 for a listing of speaking organizations).

1. PRACTICE MAKES PERFECT.

When you're already somewhat comfortable speaking to groups, but still want to hone your presentation, offer to guest-lecture at your local high school or university. Teachers and professors are usually delighted to share their classrooms with a guest expert. Then go after other nonpaid speaking engagements. Government agencies, nonprofit groups, and alumni meetings, for example, are excellent places to volunteer your speaking experience. Adult education centers and colleges are another smart choice; if they don't offer classes in your area of expertise, propose one that you could teach. You'll not only gain hours of speaking experience, but your exposure will be furthered when you and your class are mentioned in the catalog. Area businesses may also be interested in what you have to say, as may health clubs.

TEACH WHAT YOU KNOW.

You should also seek out business groups such as the Rotary Club, Chamber of Commerce, and the Kiwanis Club, as well as industry organizations. Conventions are another great place to reach large numbers of people. Look for professional gatherings whose fields are outside of, yet complementary to, your business. For instance, an attorney may want to address a convention of corrections officers, to inform them of a new law that's relevant to their rights. By doing so, the lawyer offers valuable information and also expands his client base by presenting himself as the authority on the legal rights of corrections officers.

Offer to share advice to a niche market you serve. If you design retail spaces, addressing retail associations can help increase your visibility and reputation, while simultaneously marketing your services. (See pp. 77 and 78 for a sample letter.)

2. SPEAK TO YOUR AUDIENCE.

Cynthia Vocell, a New Hampshire–based designer of upscale day spas and salons, has found that servicing a niche market lets her penetrate it more easily and quickly than a broad-based market. Vocell, because of her writing and speaking engagements, has become known as an authority on servicing the salon owner. "Opportunities have arisen where they wouldn't have if I didn't specialize....The value of niche marketing is that it allows you to procure a better client every couple of years because you've become an expert in the field, and businesses that are higher up in the ladder begin to notice you. If I hadn't specialized, I wouldn't be working with the caliber of clients I now have."

Exhibitions and trade shows also provide excellent opportunities to spread the word about your product or service. Just make sure to contact the trade-show company six to twelve months in advance to arrange your speaking engagement.

Then, send new and prospective clients custom invitations to your speech.

Not only do trade shows and exhibitions promote your product or service; they also present an ideal time to take the media to lunch, or to schedule brief meetings with them. You can also send pre- and post-event mailings to the press, to alert them to your presence at the show.

Clubs devoted to singles and hobbyists should also be checked out—especially if you're a member. When they have one of their regularly scheduled meetings, you may be just the speaker they're looking for.

Sometimes the darndest places offer opportunities to speak in person. TomTom, an innovative restaurant in Washington, D.C., has an artist-in-residence program. In addition to serving affordable tapas and pizzas, the restaurant provides platforms where artists can craft their products and talk informally, while patrons watch. "You can make and sell your product while people are dining," says Steve Latour, who demonstrates lei-making. "I always wanted to be the Frank Perdue of leis," says this petal-pusher.

Still at a loss about where to speak? You may want to host your own event. For instance, if you own a residential real-estate firm, you might invite past, current, and potential clients to a seminar on trends in real estate sales and leases. By extending a special invitation, and providing information on a one-on-one basis, you'll increase your visibility to clients and also reinforce your value to them.

SPEAK ABOUT WHAT YOU KNOW, TO THOSE WHO WANT TO KNOW.

Speaking, by its own merit, does wonders for your reputation, but you can hardly consider it free publicity. After all, you invest your time, words, and wit every time you take the stage. That's why it's important to approach each occasion as a marketing opportunity.

Where Speaking Opportunities Exist:

Adult education centers
Professional organizations
Industry associations
Trade shows
Corporations/local businesses
High school or college classes
Government/not-for-profit
   organizations

Rotary Clubs
Chamber of Commerce meetings
Alumni meetings
Clubs for singles and hobbyists
Health clubs
Restaurants
Host your own meetings

Audio/Visual Checklist:

☑ Slide projector with remote control,
   zoom lenses, automatic focus set-up
   OR
☑ Overhead projector

☑ One large 8-ft x 8-ft screen
☑ 8-ft materials table
☑ One flip chart with ample paper and
   colored markers

3. MAXIMIZE EVERY SPEAKING ENGAGEMENT.

Since public speaking does wonders for your reputation, here's how to make the most of each speaking engagement. First, prior to each, request that the organization send out information about you on a flyer that bears your photograph and a brief description of your speaking topic. Or make sure that the flyers are handed out before you take the stage. (You may want to do it yourself, and simply ask the organization to reimburse you. After all, you are also promoting your host organization.) By doing so, you make people aware of your name and pave the way for a good turnout. The picture is especially important; the Public Relations Society of America estimates that a photo increases by 80 percent the likelihood that your flyer will be read!

GET MENTIONED IN THE HOST ORGANIZATION'S DIRECT-MAIL EFFORTS.

Send press releases to the consumer and trade press, informing the public about your upcoming appearance; make sure to extend a special invitation to reporters you've previously worked with, or hope will show up. You may even want to barter advertising space in trade publications and offer your speech for free, in exchange for free advertising in the host's program guide, newsletter, or publication. In addition, ask the host organization for a list of attendees and their addresses, so you can add them to your mailing list.

PUBLICIZE YOUR ENGAGEMENT.

In addition, to get the word out about your appearance, advertise the date of your speech in the local newspaper or trade publication; and offer to write a separate article for the host's newsletter. If you actually do get paid, make sure to donate the amount to your favorite charity; it will foster even more goodwill for your business and possibly generate separate press coverage of its own. Just send a photo and a press release describing the event, amount of your donation, name of the charity, and other details to your local newspaper. Also mention it in your newsletter for even more exposure.

LEVERAGE YOUR EXPOSURE.

Make sure to record your speech. Afterward, listen to it, transcribe it, and discern how you could have made it even better. It might even inspire new ideas on how to market your business.

After you've finished speaking, make sure that your audience receives a workbook, a special handout containing some of the information you've talked about, or ad specialty items, such as T-shirts, mugs, pens, or memo pads, with your name and logo on them. The more clever you are, the better; every time your audience sees or uses this item, they will think of you, and a more inspired idea will practically guarantee that you and your company will be remembered.

LEAVE THEM WITH SOMETHING TO REMEMBER YOU BY.

You might also give your audience a current copy of your newsletter. Also make sure to exchange business cards; this way, you can add names to your mailing list, and they will have your address when they need a speaker.

After you've successfully finished a speaking engagement, or have completed a writing assignment, you may receive rave reviews from your audience. If so, get testimonials. Ask everyone if they might put their comments on paper, so you can use their comments in your marketing. Third-party endorsements can't be beat.

GET IT IN WRITING.

The more you stand in front of an audience and share your expertise, the stronger your business will grow. In addition, chances are you will feel more confident and powerful about yourself and your business—not a bad advantage!

PRACTICE MAKES PERFECT.

Now that you write and speak like a pro, it's time to get the word out even more. The next chapter discusses how to accent your expertise.

SAMPLE LETTER TO REQUEST SPEAKING ENGAGEMENTS

Date

Contact
Program Director
Center for Women & Enterprise
Boston, MA

Dear Contact:

It was a pleasure to meet with you and Andrea Silbert last week to discuss ways we might work together in the future. I'm happy that we're planning a full-day workshop for the fall.

As I mentioned, I'm happy to do whatever it takes to entice a sponsor to support this presentation and add value to the participating sponsor and each participant.

I've also enclosed a sampling of letters that I have received since my appearance at Inc. World last year. I'm certain these would be helpful, to show a potential sponsor the long-standing value their direct association with this presentation would have on participants as well as their prospective customers. I've also included a copy of *How to Be a Big Fish in Any Pond* for you to have to show to potential sponsors.

Benefits to the sponsor would include:

- Sponsor(s) customized version of *How to Be a Big Fish in Any Pond* two-cassette audiotape program and 56-page resource guide with sponsor's logo—valued at $69.95, to be provided to each participant @ $49.95 (anticipated attendance 50–100)
- Appearance at sponsor(s) booth for product signings
- Sponsor letter to be included in each *How to Be a Big Fish in Any Pond* program

- Sponsor acknowledgment on-site during introduction, conclusion, and via on-site participant promotion tied in with the presentation (i.e., certificate of completion, etc.)
- Signage
- Mention in direct-mail efforts (Impression Impact newsletter, *MarketAbility* (2,500), Center for Women & Enterprise direct-mail effort)

A participating sponsor should also be encouraged to tag their existing advertising with a mention of the seminar for additional visibility.

Caitlin, once again, I enjoyed coming in to meet with you and Andrea to discuss working with the Center for Women & Enterprise. Please call me if you have any questions at (508) 287-0718. I look forward to talking with you soon.

Best regards,

Nancy Michaels

cc: Andrea C. Silbert,

Chief Executive Officer/Co-founder

Enclosures

Eight

ACCENTUATE YOUR EXPERTISE

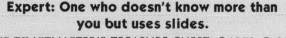

Expert: One who doesn't know more than you but uses slides.
THE TOASTMASTER'S TREASURE CHEST, ©1979, P. 388

1. Promote yourself on a bigger radar screen.
2. Enter or establish a contest.
3. List yourself as an expert.

Victoria MacKenzie-Childs had a problem. During the summer months, her New York City boutique—like most shops on Madison Avenue—was lacking customers. So this designer of whimsical housewares—who typically dresses in costumes and paints her hair in a rainbow of colors—decided to stage a parade down the city sidewalks, to attract attention to her offbeat store. First, MacKenzie-Childs outfitted her staff in fanciful costumes; they morphed into giant plates, vases, tassels, acrobats, nymphs, and cheerleaders. Then she had them march and sing down Madison and Fifth Avenues, handing out postcards and photographs, and inviting people into the boutique. "It has made *everyone* come to our store," exclaims MacKenzie-Childs. Now, four years later, the "promenade" is widely anticipated and enormously popular. "Everyone says, 'Yeah, MacKenzie-Childs!' There's no reason for retail *not* to be out in the world," she explains. "But the higher the rent, the more restrained people become," she adds. "If we hadn't done 'the promenade,' we would have otherwise been a quaint little shop on an elitist corner of the world. We are a store on Madison Avenue that says, 'Welcome.'"

MacKenzie-Childs understands that getting noticed is the name of the game. The secret is to get yourself on a bigger radar screen—in any way possible—to strut your stuff and showcase your business in a complementary way.

1. PROMOTE YOURSELF ON A BIGGER RADAR SCREEN.

That's exactly what Bill Kickham did. An attorney based in Westwood, Massachusetts, Kickham knew that he needed to set himself apart from other lawyers in his area. But how? The answer came one day when he received his cable TV bill in the mail. He wound up pitching a "news you can use" legal show called *At the Bar*, which he now tapes about once a month, with him as a host. Though Kickham isn't paid for his services, the visibility has been great. It has led him to lucrative opportunities with new clients, increased credibility with his existing clients, his own legal-advice column in the local newspaper, and even a national TV appearance as a legal analyst on *Court TV*.

HOLD A DEMONSTRATION, WORKSHOP, OR CLASS

Other ways to give away some of your knowledge? Sponsor free in-store events in which you share your expertise. A hardware store, for example, could offer classes in home decorating or home repair. Beauty salons could hold complimentary sessions on hair care and blow-drying techniques. A resume service might offer a free seminar on how to write a good resume, with discounts available for customers who use its service. Likewise, a temporary employment agency might teach a special class on tax savings for freelancers.

OFFER FREE INFORMATION THROUGH FLYERS

If no one positions you as an expert when you desperately want the attention—do it yourself! How? By adding valuable information to all of your written sales tools.

That's what Beverly Martin of Windham, New Hampshire, did. Martin, a professional seamstress, printed up colorful flyers about her custom-made headpieces, which she handed out at bridal shows. However, she also took the savvy tactic of showing four drawings of face shapes, and the headpiece that would flatter each the best; this simple measure established her as a headpiece expert in the minds of potential customers. Martin also included renderings of four body shapes, and the gowns best for each. Instead of an advertisement that might ordinarily be tossed in the wastebasket, Martin's flyer wound up being a service-oriented marketing tool filled with practical information. "Brides hang onto it, even fifteen months later," says Martin. "After they read it, brides figure that I must know how to help them make a headpiece selection."

2. ENTER OR ESTABLISH A CONTEST.

Fred Levine, a New Hampshire–based video producer, got an idea to create a children's video after watching his two sons riveted to the TV set while viewing a segment on road construction on *Sesame Street*. As a result, Levine wrote, produced, and shot a video on the same subject, but had no luck advertising it. Exasperated, Levine sought out awards competitions sponsored by parenting and children's organizations, in the hope of achieving recognition by winning an award. During the following year, *Road Construction Ahead* won several awards, and Levine used this information, plus snippets of favorable reviews, in his subsequent ads. The result? Levine sold so many tapes during the holidays that he had to hire temporary workers to come in and answer the phones.

Every actor knows that winning an Oscar paves the way for making better movies, earning bigger salaries, and providing more career opportunities. Those advantages can be easily translated to your industry by simply winning an award. The right kudos can be a kick in the pants to your salability! It can also translate into free publicity; winning an industry or small business award practically assures that your picture will wind up in the newspaper, and that you'll be sought out on the public-speaking circuit.

Inventor Joy Mangano knows all about it. If you ever watch television, chances are you've seen her and her Miracle Mop. In 1995 Mangano's commercial was awarded as the Best Short-Form Commercial by the National Infomercial Marketing Association, augmenting her credibility even more. Let's face it, having an unbiased group bestow an award on you or your business is another great way to make others notice.

Does seeking out awards sound too tedious? Then leave it up to your vendors. But first get them excited about the product.

That's the marketing miracle that happened with the ergonomically correct Sensa pen. Created in 1995 by entrepreneur Boyd Willat, Sensa—a unique pen with a cushioned Plasmium grip—has received numerous awards, thanks to its many vendors. One of them, who was a member of the Industrial Designers Society of America, entered the pen in the Society's annual design contest. It wound up winning the Silver Industrial Design Award in the same year. Also in 1995, the Sensa pen was featured in a contemporary design exhibit at New York's Museum of Modern Art; the museum's gift shop carried the pen, and a salesperson, who knew of the upcoming event, excitedly brought the pen to the attention of the exhibit designers. The rest is history. Even the unusual packaging has won design awards—each box is a combination business-card holder, pen rest, and carrying case. Those awards came about because the designers submitted their designs to the appropriate committees. The secret here? "Get your vendors excited.

The more you generate buzz about your product, the more buzz is created," says Joan E. Meijer, spokesperson for Sensa. "Credibility is good for the bottom line."

Sensa also lets the product demonstrate itself. Willat realized that most stores that carried Sensa pens had customers who paid for them with credit cards. And what do credit cards require? A signature with a pen. So he and his designers created an illustrated counter display that is meant to sit next to the cash register. It features a pen, a pad, and a sign that says, "Dare to feel the world's most comfortable pen." Meijer says that this marketing ploy alone was a stroke of genius that blew all sales out of the water.

GET YOUR VENDORS EXCITED.

How to find out about contests? Search for those sponsored by organizations and associations that you belong to, as well as those that are compatible in your field. Attend meetings and conferences, and study the "announcements" sections of professional journals. You just might find notices of upcoming contests!

Check pages 105 and 106 for a definitive list of entrepreneurial awards sponsored by the Small Business Administration, various small business magazines, and organizations like the Horatio Alger Society. Whatever you do, don't be modest about your accomplishments. Everyone likes doing business with a winner!

"I'D LIKE TO THANK . . ."

Barry Potekin knows about the advantages of winning awards. In 1996 his company, Gold Coast Dogs, won one of the Blue Chip Enterprise Initiative awards sponsored by Connecticut

Mutual Life Insurance and the U.S. Chamber of Commerce. Although two hundred small businesses are selected annually, only fifty appear on USA Network's small-business morning newscast, *First Business*. Gold Coast Dogs was also one of only four businesses further honored at the U.S. Chamber of Commerce's annual meeting; their stories are also featured in the annual April issue of *Nation's Business* magazine, and they also receive additional local publicity. The advantages of winning? He says that he eats better, adding that he has also been broke, but he votes for having money. Potekin has also been entered into the Entrepreneur Hall of Fame at the University of Illinois.

HOLD A CONTEST

Another way to propel yourself into recognition as a professional expert is to hold contests in which you are the judge and thus give, not receive, the awards. For example, a bakery might sponsor a contest for the most beautifully decorated birthday cake or an architectural firm might hold an amateur home-design contest. Picking the winner not only makes you into an expert; it also lends itself to a photo opportunity for all newspapers.

Yomega, a yo-yo company based in Fall River, Massachusetts, has reaped great success with this idea. They sponsor events and contests for their retailers, and give away yo-yos as prizes, which results in great word-of-mouth advertising. In Fall 1999, they even sponsored a three-day event in Providence. Do these events improve the bottom line? "Absolutely," says Jane Howes, publicist. "It promotes the spirit of yo-yo-playing and keeps it alive." One of their employees, Chris Ciosek, is even the Guinness world-record holder, having performed thirty yo-yo tricks in one minute.

Yomega also decorated a van into a "moving billboard" that, at this writing, is making a five-city tour that has generated awareness in the *Washington Post*, and on TV's *Fox and Friends*.

3. LIST YOURSELF AS AN EXPERT.

You also can't beat buying an ad and listing yourself as an expert in publications such as *Radio-TV Interview Report* or *Yearbook of Experts, Authorities and Spokespersons*, which are distributed to media nationwide (see pp. 106 and 107). Romance author Greg Godek says, "I take out ads all of the time in the *Radio-TV Interview Report* and I do awesome with it."

At this point you should be well on your way to being acknowledged as an expert in your field. Now you're ready to add "star quality" to your already impeccable credentials. But one of you may not be enough to go around—that's where our version of "cloning" comes in, complete with videotapes, workbooks, infomercials, and the Internet.

NiNe

PACK A PUNCH WITH PERSONAL PROMOTION

**America made me a multimillionaire....
The beauty of this country is that people listen to
me and pay for my advice.**
BEVERLY HILLS DESIGNER BIJAN, IN *THE ROBB REPORT*, FEBRUARY 1987

1. Become a "personality" and appear in your own advertising.
2. Be the star of your own TV or radio show.
3. Leverage your celebrity status.

Ready to play a word association game? Who do you think of when you hear the words "popcorn"..."fried chicken"...and "Stop the Insanity!"? If you answered Orville Redenbacher, Colonel Sanders, and Susan Powter, you're absolutely right.

As these entrepreneurs might tell you, it's downright lucrative to become the star of your own show. Putting your face in front of your product and becoming personally involved in your marketing efforts is an effective way to promote your business.

Why? Because people tend to feel better about a product or service when they can associate it with it a real-live human being—and someone they can relate to. It inspires trust and confidence. When consumers feel they have a personal connection with the big kahuna at the top—meaning you—they may be more apt to buy your product or service, and not that of the faceless competition. And, heaven forbid, should anything go wrong, they know, from the outset, who to complain to.

Remember, you don't need mountains of money to promote your business—in some cases all it requires is ingenuity, a sincere belief in what you do, and some pizzazz and personality. Here's how to do it.

1. BECOME A "PERSONALITY" AND APPEAR IN YOUR OWN ADVERTISING.

Jim McCann, the brains behind 1-800-FLOWERS, knows all about the importance of appearing in his own advertising. As he says in *What's Luck Got to Do with It,*[1] "As a brand name, 1-800-FLOWERS is as anonymous as it gets and ours is a personal business. Appearing in ads allowed me to say, 'We are real. This really is a family business. I really am a florist.' This in turn enabled our phone number to stand for 'I'm sorry,' 'Congratulations,' or 'Happy Valentine's Day.'" The flowers may be telemarketed, but the service is strictly personal.

Becoming a "personality" is one of the savviest things an entrepreneur can do. While this tactic isn't for everyone—because, after all, you do sacrifice some of your privacy—it works wonders for individuals who like the limelight. It can be exciting, fun, interesting, and downright lucrative.

What does it take?

- A willingness to go public and give up some of your privacy
- Self-confidence and a healthy ego

---

[1] John Wiley & Sons, Inc., 1997, chap. 2.

- An ability to show your personality—and the more unique it is, the better
- A desire to cultivate a following and fans
- An ability to take criticism
- An enjoyment of visibility and power

What are the benefits?

- Instills consumer confidence
- Creates instant name recognition/awareness
- Personalizes the product or service
- Inspires trust and confidence
- Creates a larger-than-life persona
- Gives people a favorable impression of you and your business

Inventor Joy Mangano got herself on QVC and the rest is history. Before QVC, Mangano sold her Miracle Mop to catalogs and retailers and did as many demonstrations as possible. "Demonstrations are important, and people love it," Mangano says. Back in 1990, though, when she started her business "from a desk in my bedroom," she says, people didn't want to pay twenty dollars for a mop. "It was very, very disheartening," Mangano adds. The turning point occurred when she brought the Miracle Mop to QVC and met with a buyer, who agreed to purchase a small quantity. The mop appeared on the air with a QVC host. It didn't sell well and QVC was ready to return them. Then Mangano convinced the senior executives to let *her* appear *live* on the air, to demonstrate the Miracle Mop. Her vivacious presence and enthusiasm inspired callers to buy thousands in less than ten minutes. Mangano believes that these live testimonials made her the multimillion-dollar success story that she is—whereas many TV sales programs, says Mangano, cause customers to question the honesty of callers. In her case, however, "people see the credibility, plus I'm there as the inventor of the product."

At this writing, Mangano appears in her own hour-long program on QVC, *Make Your Space a Better Place,* and has also appeared on a shopping channel in England. "People come up to me; I can't even go to a mall anymore," says Mangano. "They say, 'I love you and your commercial.'"

Attorney Jim Sokolove is another example; he is well known to Boston audiences for his slogan, "Don't go it alone." Sokolove began advertising on TV in 1980 before it was commonplace for law firms, and hired an actor to do the announcing. "But focus groups said that they wanted to see someone younger who's behind the business," says Sokolove. "That's what got me into acting as the spokesperson. Our ads became twice as effective immediately and we got more business." Sokolove admits, however, that "to some people, 'celebrity' gives you instant credibility...to others I am a negative ambulance-chaser." The TV publicity, for the most part, offered side benefits—it got him into writing bylined articles and lecturing on ethics at law schools, "positioning me as an expert on marketing legal services...It's also given me a position of status in the community," he adds.

Sy Sperling, creator of The Hair Club for Men, also appealed to his audience in an unprecedented way when he appeared in his own TV commercials, saying, "I'm not only the Hair Club president...I'm also a client." He told a trade publication, "I think that by going on TV, I personally had a lot to do with erasing the stigma attached to hair replacement. When I went on the air before millions of people, saying I'm bald, take a look at my 'before' shot, I put it on the table...when somebody in the public eye comes forward with something like that, it helps alleviate the fears of the average person."[2]

Sperling also used a brilliant marketing ploy. Although he initially called his business the Hair Replacement Center, he felt the need to remove the stigma attached to baldness. "Men with thinning hair are embarrassed," he says. That's when he decided to call his business a "club," which had none of the negative

---

[2] *Cosmetic and Drug Marketing,* Nov./Dec., 1989.

connotations. Now it was seen as an exclusive grooming club where men could go without being ashamed. "It was very simple and memorable...like Club Med," says Sperling. "I came up with the magic bullet." He adds, "I thought the 'Hair Club' would lead to publicity. It had a touch of lightness to it. (I thought that) Maybe the Lettermans and Lenos of the world would give us free publicity, and they did... I'm probably the most recognized businessman in America."

Sperling adds, "Creativity is finding a simple solution for a complex problem... 'Join the club...Hair's the key.'"

> **Points to remember:**
> - Practice what you preach.
> - Use your sense of humor.
> - Create and build membership.

2. BE THE STAR OF YOUR OWN TV OR RADIO SHOW.

Getting yourself on TV is yet another way to stand out head-and-shoulders above the competition. Local-access and cable shows, and even your local network affiliate, may be looking for someone just like you! (See p. 107 for a listing of media directories.)

Follow the example of Steve Latour of Washington, D.C., who's otherwise known as "The Lei Man." Latour sought a novel approach to market his handmade leis. He lucked out with his own public-access TV show, *Lei Man's World;* because he couldn't simply advertise his leis, Latour had to develop a concept for the show. Eventually, the program consisted of Latour and several friends reviewing food, wine, and films—while wearing Latour's unique leis. "I was looking for a cheap way to advertise," says Latour. "And I saw *Wayne's World.*" Callers who phone in give their comments on the topics—and are asked, by the way, if they want to order a lei as well.

FIND A NEED AND FILL IT

Attorney Bill Kickham of Westwood, Massachusetts, felt frustrated after receiving no response from advertising in local newspapers. "I came up with nothing. Goose egg. Zip. Zero," says Kickham. "It's hard to get clients, not to mention compete with other lawyers.... I had to differentiate myself from the herd." One day, after paying his cable TV bill, he got a brainstorm. "I thought, 'There's a potential need to educate the public on common legal problems...to get free advice. People love to get something for nothing.'"

So Kickham, whose prior experience included a stint as the on-air spokesperson and New England Regional Counsel for the Insurance Information Institute, approached his local Cablevision station with a concept for his own TV show, *At The Bar*. He showed his proposal to the programming manager; within a month Kickham was on the air. The program features one guest per show and deals with consumer and criminal problems, accidents, commercial transactions, drunk driving, and more.

At this writing, the four-year-old show has received such a good response that Kickham (and news about his show) were featured on the front page of his local newspaper, and Kickham has been approached to expand into other markets. The show generates business for him, and he frequently gets recognized on the street. "My primary objective is to generate business and use the show as a segue to be a local reporter," Kickham says. His plan has already started to work: Kickham recently made a national appearance as a legal analyst on *Court TV* in New York City.

When Kickham's TV audition tape is ready, he plans to send it out to TV stations—accompanied by a fake subpoena. "That's sure to get someone's attention," Kickham adds.

Kelvin Boston of Detroit, Michigan, did practically the same thing when he founded Boston Media. Boston started out as a financial planner for American Express Financial Advisors, but left because he wanted to reach out more to minorities and middle-income Americans. He started his own production company and got on local-access TV in Detroit with his show, *The Color of Money*. Guests included bankers and lawyers. After six months, the show did so well that it received "local origination" status, meaning that they finally got a real set! After a banker was bombarded with calls after an appearance, a local bank sponsored the show. Next, Boston looked into syndication but found it too expensive, so he self-syndicated; he attended public-television meetings, wrote to public-television stations across the country, and sent his favorable reviews to PBS stations nation-wide. The strategy worked. At one point, as many as 110 stations carried it. (Program syndication resources are listed on p. 107.)

Eventually Boston pulled the plug on the show, as it tended to attract young viewers—the wrong demographics. In 1996 he wrote the book *Smart Money Moves for African-Americans*, and retitled the show the same. Now he's launching a national magazine and a radio show. "Every time someone hears the name you get more bang for the buck," he says.

WAYNE'S WORLD REVISITED: HOW TO BREAK INTO LOCAL TV AS A HOST

No doubt about it—having your own TV show can boost business. But how to break in? First, watch local cable and public-access shows to see what is or isn't being covered. Then, define your area of expertise. What type of show could you bring to TV that isn't currently being aired? In other words, find a need and fill it. What are your unique talents? Perhaps you have a gift for gab and a spontaneous sense of humor. Both are assets for TV!

Brainstorm show and concept ideas. What is the tone of your proposed show? How is it special or different from other shows that are already out there? Then, write a proposal to the manager of your local-access station. Show tapes of any previous TV work.

HOW TO BREAK IN AS A GUEST

It's not that different from breaking in as a host. The same rules apply, but it may be easier breaking into cable or public-access TV than into your local VHF talk show.

Here's how to start. If you've been quoted for your expertise in any print media, dovetail off of that. Send copies of the publicity to the producer, with a sheet explaining the kinds of shows your expertise could fit into. For example, after Karpowicz wrote *I Love Men in Tasseled Loafers*, she appeared on TV talk shows that focused on dating; auditioned for *The Dating Game;*

and spoke about love, dating, and relationships on radio shows on Valentine's Day.

After identifying your expertise, list the TV and radio shows where your expertise might apply. Call the shows and get a listing of upcoming programs—perhaps you can simply plug yourself into one that's already scheduled. Don't forget seasonal topics: diet and weight loss topics fit into January and New Year's resolutions as well as June and swimsuit season, wedding expertise is ideal for June, and romance is ripe in February for Valentine's Day. (See p. 107 for resource listings.)

3. LEVERAGE YOUR CELEBRITY STATUS.

After an appearance, get videotapes and audiotapes of your performance, which you can make duplicates of and send to other potential media outlets. If you have a newsletter, make sure to mention all of your appearances, both before and after the fact. In fact, make sure to promote all of your upcoming performances in your newsletter. You should also consider sending postcards announcing your appearances to clients, business prospects, and other media.

In Honolulu, Richard Field, owner of a gourmet store, also found that making himself into a celebrity set his business apart. After appearing on a local radio talk show, where he spoke about marrying wine and food, "We got so many calls and reactions that the producer wanted to know if it could be done weekly." Today Field hosts his own weekly radio show, *In Good Taste,* where he educates people about food, wine, cigars, and cognac. "What's been amazing is that I thought that if I'm lucky, it would take one, two, or three years to get a response. Actually, within six weeks we *knew* we were getting a tremendous response," Field says. How did he know? For one thing, after each show, when his store offered free samples, it was inundated with shoppers. Furthermore, food sales significantly increased, and are today almost equal to the strong sales of cigars and wine. "It helped all across the board," says Field, whose show has attracted superchefs such as Jacques Pepin and Jeremiah Tower.

"Those names started a snowball effect for us, and made the show a profit-center," says Field, who even starred in an American Express advertisement.

Field also employed another tactic to set his business apart. Bear in mind that being a purveyor of gourmet food in Hawaii, where Spam is enormously popular, is a hard sell. "This is not the gourmet capital of the world," says Field, who found that "consumers in Hawaii tend to buy what's advertised. . . . Here, people focus on brand names." But Field utilized what he refers to as "contrary marketing," in which "our strategy is to find products that are much more interesting." Field works with local farmers who grow first-rate produce. "We like to look for products in our backyard that are world-class." He's been at the forefront with Hawaiian Vintage Chocolate—the only chocolate grown in the United States (on the Big Island)—and also with tomatoes, lettuces, and even locally made sausages. "I go to the farmers and keep hounding them," says Field. "Then, we go to the local press and say, 'Look what this farmer is doing'…then we make stars out of them."

Points to remember:

- Start out small.
- Snowball your success.
- Be contrary; sail against the wind.

After you've reaped the success of personal promotion, it's time to ensure that your products and services are in two places at once! The next chapter, "Clone Yourself," will show you how to make the most of The Brand Called *You*.

TeN

CLONE YOURSELF

Fame is a magnifying glass.
ENGLISH PROVERB

1. Create products that sell when you're asleep.
2. Demonstrate your product on an infomercial.
3. Get Web connected.

Savvy marketers say that it's smart to explore numerous opportunities, so that their product or service is in two places at once. And if *you* can still be selling, even when you're asleep, that's even better. But how? With an instructional audiotape, videotape, and workbook, that's how! Each can help you promote your business, bring in additional income, and allow you to reach customers who may not have the budget to hire you. These products also have the advantage of adding to your credibility.

1. CREATE PRODUCTS THAT SELL WHEN YOU'RE ASLEEP.

Audiotapes are an excellent way to clone yourself. Tape one of your speeches and use it as your product. Or, hire the services of a recording studio to tape scripted material (see p. 105 for more information). In this day and age, when people practically live in their cars, audiotapes are a smart tool. Just ask Deepak Chopra!

Workbooks can stand on their own as take-home items that your audience can do on their own, or as reinforcement to be used while you give a speech. To produce one, simply transcribe your information and add worksheets, checklists, and exercises.

Or try a videotape. Naturally, not all businesses lend themselves to videotape, but you may be surprised at how many do. A dog-trainer's videotape can show obedience-training techniques; a financial advisor's, investing tips. With the right videotape, your business could achieve Jane Fonda–like proportions! If you decide to produce a tape, enlist the help of a professionally run studio. Your aim is to create a high-quality product that will hold up under repeated playings.

Denie Schach swears that her infomercial videotape made her invention, the Hairdini, a success. Timing also helped. Schach introduced her product, which helps women to put up their hair into various French twists, at a time when it was all the rage. "Updos were popular," says Schach. The Hairdini was very successful on QVC, but Schach wanted to reach a different pool of customers. So she paid a media buyer and produced a half-hour infomercial. "It tested fabulous," says Schach. "The Hairdini was a total winner. Besides, it was such a demonstratable product," she adds.

INFORMATION + ADVERTISING = INFOMERCIAL

2. DEMONSTRATE YOUR PRODUCT ON AN INFOMERCIAL.

Schach got another brainstorm: She also produced an educational video that would teach women exactly how to use the Hairdini. She spent $40,000 of her profits and produced continuous-play videotapes, which she gave to all of her retailers. When played in-store, "it stopped people and got their attention," Schach says. "I taught women how to use the Hairdini by simply putting it on videotape."

LIGHTS! CAMERA! ACTION!

Remember that snow-vaporizer of yours? The one you demonstrated on B-Roll and sent to news stations across the country? Well, it's time to showcase your invention before a broader, larger audience. You could take out a print ad in a national publication—*Alaska* magazine, maybe? Or how about *Snow Country*? But remember, your product just begs a hands-on demonstration. A television commercial would be nice, but you really need more time to show off all of your snow-vaporizer's features. If you could only buy a half-hour commercial....

Actually, you can. It's called an infomercial—the pseudo-television shows made popular by Ron Popeil, inventor of such gadgets as the Pocket Fisherman and GLH-9—the canned "great looking hair" you spray-paint onto your bald head.

Unfortunately, the days of low-budget "it slices, it dices" programs are over. If you want to make an infomercial, you'll pay a small fortune, because these days slick production values and top-name stars rule the paid programming airwaves.

"This industry is maturing. In the beginning there were lots of wild-card successes," said Meg Hill, head of development for Shulberg Mediaworks, a San Francisco production house, which has written, directed, and/or produced such infomercials as "Personal Power" with Anthony Robbins and "Making Love Work" with Barbara DeAngelis. Now everyone from Microsoft to presidential candidates have discovered the potential of the thirty-minute televised sales pitch, driving up the cost of airtime.

Here's what you can expect to spend, according to the National Infomercial Marketing Association (NIMA) in Washington, D.C. The average cost to produce a thirty-minute show is $250,000. This is what a reputable infomercial ad agency will charge to write the script, hire actors, and tape the show. Media test marketing will run about $30,000. The cost of hiring a telemarketer to handle incoming calls is $2,000 to $5,000. Buying airtime will cost $50,000 a month, minimum, $500,000 average. Other considerations include fulfillment and shipping.

And if that's not discouraging, estimates place the success ratio of infomercials between 1 in 12 and 1 in 20. "It's high risk with the potential of incredibly high return," said Tim Hawthorne, co-founder of NIMA and chairman of Hawthorne Communications, a direct-response advertising agency based in Fairfield, Iowa.

If you're determined to get your snow-vaporizer on the air but can't seem to raise the cash, a production house may invest in your product. However, it will also keep most of the profits, leaving you with 5 to 6 percent.

WHAT MAKES A GOOD INFOMERCIAL?

Hawthorne recommends the following:

- Television is a mass medium, so the product should have mass appeal. An infomercial on a niche product is doomed to failure. (Fitness, health, beauty, and diet products account for nearly half of all infomercial sales.)
- The product should have a markup of 5 to 1.
- The product should be demonstrable.
- You should have convincing testimonials from people who have used the product and fallen in love with it.

When looking for an agency to produce your infomercial, choose one with plenty of experience—at least five years in business and five productions under its belt. Hawthorne's firm produced the fourth infomercial to hit the airwaves after federal programming guidelines opened the doors for paid programming in 1984. Its clients include such Fortune 500 accounts as Black & Decker, Nissan, and Apple, yet its success ratio is between 35 and 50 percent. "Don't even dream of going with someone who doesn't have significant experience. You're wasting your time and your money," Hawthorne said.

For more information call the National Infomercial Marketing Association. (See resources on p. 105.)

SHOP TILL YOU DROP—AND DON'T STOP!

If you think your product is a star, try debuting it in front of 140 million households. That's the combined viewership of the nation's top two television retailers—QVC and the Home Shopping Network. Each program has a formal procedure for product submissions, both of which begin with your request for a vendor packet. The packet includes an application and instructions for submissions. (See p. 105 for addresses and phone numbers.)

QVC IS A-OK!

QVC prefers photos to actual product samples. A merchandise buyer will review your application. If they're interested, they'll request a sample. This must pass what QVC calls its "rigorous Quality Assurance requirements." If approved, they request that all products be individually packaged, labeled, and shipped to a QVC warehouse to ensure their seven- to ten-day delivery guarantee to customers.

QVC accepts a wide variety of goods but will not accept junior apparel, furs and fur-related items, guns and gun-related items, subscriptions, personalized items, 900 phone programs, service-related products, and novelty shirts and sweatshirts. QVC likes to offer exclusive product launches as well as unique products offered for the first time.

Their programming is thematic. Product selections are based on how they will segment within broadcast programs, so it's a good idea to look at their schedule to see where your item fits in.

First-time orders at QVC usually range between $10,000 and $15,000 wholesale.

HOME SWEET HOME SHOPPING NETWORK

HSN prefers photos, brochures, and/or catalogs to the actual item. The network won't return unsolicited examples and will return solicited examples at the vendor's expense. If you give an item's retail value, you must substantiate your claim by one or more of the following:

- Current national catalog ad
- Comparative shopping survey
- Manufacturer's current price list showing MSRP for the exact item
- Letter from the manufacturer or their national distributor

After HSN receives your paperwork and a photo of the product, your materials will be reviewed by its Merchandising Department to determine whether it is appropriate for on-air sales. If it is, HSN will contact you to schedule an appointment with the appropriate buyer. If an agreement is made, HSN will issue a purchase order for the product. HSN then expects you to deliver your product to its warehouse, where they will hold it before presenting it on air. (See p. 105 for more information on HSN.)

WHAT IF BEING A RECOGNIZED CELEBRITY IS NOT FOR YOU?

Jim Koch (pronounced "Cook"), founder of The Boston Beer Company that makes Samuel Adams beer, prefers some anonymity. Koch's voice can be heard on the radio airwaves and he wouldn't have it any other way. "No one could speak with more passion and love for Samuel Adams than me," says Koch. "I speak with authority and authenticity because I know and believe in my product completely."

Koch initially advertised via radio because of its affordability; however, today, with awards and rave reviews for The Boston Beer Company under his belt, he prefers to stick with radio. "I'm a real person with a real life and being easily recognized would be intrusive," he says.

Koch adds that being his own company spokesperson has been an advantage. The effect of his "personality" on the bottom line? "It conveys my passion and the authenticity of Sam Adams Beer."

TRY RADIO IF YOU DON'T WANT INSTANT RECOGNITION.

3. GET WEB CONNECTED.

As a small business owner, going on-line can be the lifeline that keeps your business afloat. The Internet is mind-boggling in its potential to reach huge numbers of far-flung customers. Yet its capacity to gobble up hours of precious time is just as astounding.

Before launching your Internet marketing strategy, determine your goals and plot out the most efficient way to accomplish them. Here are some ways to tap the Internet's potential without zapping your resources.

PUBLISH A WORLD WIDE WEB PAGE

Everybody has one, it seems. And the more home pages floating around in cyberspace, the greater the need to make yours stand out. You can build your own web page either by learning the HTML programming language, or by using a software program, such as Microsoft's Front Page. But remember, your page is a reflection of your company. Do you have the artistic talent to create a visually compelling site? If not, hire someone to do it for you. It's easy to get so caught up in the look of your page that you skim over the content. Yet it's information that draws visitors, not your flashy graphics and animated logo. Following are some suggestions:

- List your company name and a brief description of what you do.
- Post customer testimonials, which add credibility.
- Include a survey on your site and offer customers an incentive to fill it out, such as a chance to win a free sample of your product or service.
- Include in your survey lines for name, address, e-mail, and phone number. Collect these for your database. You can also build your database by including a "guest book" on your site where first-time visitors can register.
- Use your site to promote yourself as an expert. Host discussions on topics related to your industry or post articles that you have written.
- Include contact information on each page of your site. This should include a mailing address, e-mail, phone number, and the name of the contact person.
- Include a listing of your products or services (and prices) as well as an order form.
- Always check your grammar. Typos, misspellings, and poor grammar make your company appear amateurish. So, just as you would double- and triple-check the copy of your traditional marketing materials, be sure to apply your editor's keen eye to your Web copy.
- Link your site with Internet search engines.

E-MAIL

Direct marketing through e-mail is risky business. What on-line user hasn't felt the sting of disappointment to discover that their "new mail" was only a sales pitch for organic dog food (and they don't even have a pet!).

To market via e-mail without alienating potential customers, target your pitches to your existing client base or to people who have requested information about your product or service. Encourage this by including your e-mail address on all of your marketing materials, with an invitation to contact you electronically for more information.

Construct your pitch itself like you would any direct-mail piece by doing the following:

- Write a punchy headline.
- Keep the message short and to the point. Include a call to action.
- Emphasize benefits over features.
- Check your grammar.
- Keep your subject line to two or three words, which is the maximum many e-mail programs will display.
- Include instructions on how to be removed from your mailing list.

NEWSGROUPS

The Internet is truly global in its reach, yet humans, social creatures that we are, crave the intimacy of smaller groups. So, we tend to form villages. The on-line equivalent of these are discussion groups, usenet groups, chats, and on-line forums. These communities are a wonderful place to network—better in some ways than traditional networking gatherings because there are no physical barriers to interfere with a meeting-of-the-minds. When you're on-line, you have no way of knowing that the person asking your advice on dealing with a problem employee is a bank president. At a Chamber of Commerce "after 5" you may never hear about a powerful female executive's problem, because you're too intimidated to approach her.

Although these cyber-villages provide ample networking opportunities, blatant marketing is discouraged. You can, however, get the word out about your business by becoming a presence in these groups. As with any social gathering, your occupation is bound to come up...so always sign-off with your "signature," which can include a brief description of your business. As people get to know you, they'll naturally feel comfortable doing business with you.

A more direct way to market yourself through discussion groups is to become a sysop, or "systems operator." These are the people who facilitate discussion and make sure things run smoothly. David Lakhani of Boise, Idaho, is a sysop on two CompuServe forums—one devoted to public relations and marketing, the other to entrepreneurship.

"It gives me a lot of incredible credibility in a community," says Lakhani, who owns Direct Hit Marketing, a full-service marketing and advertising firm and The Small Business Network, a business consulting firm. Lakhani can spend up to one hour a day on-line. His efforts have gained him clients from Chicago, Seattle, Portland, and New York, not to mention a lot of publicity (news reports often solicit sources on-line).

You can become a sysop by approaching one of the forum leaders, who will then put you through a screening process. If you prove yourself an expert in your industry, you're on-line. You can find a group to moderate by checking out the forums on the on-line services, such as America Online and CompuServe. Also, look up the Web sites of business magazines, industry or trade associations, vendors, suppliers, and small business groups. Often these include discussion groups.

As a small business owner, the global economy may not seem as immediate a concern to you, as it is to, say, General Motors. But when you consider the far-reaching marketing potential of the Internet, the prospect of introducing your product or service worldwide is not as remote as it seems.

The beauty of being the star of your own show is that, along with making yourself into a celebrity with credibility, you're also improving the bottom line. However, if that's still not enough, or if you like to take bold risks, the next chapter is for you. It's all about Madcap Marketing—employing wild, crazy, and zany tactics to attract attention and make your company stand out from the competition.

PART THREE RESOURCES:

AUDIO PRODUCTION
Moore Communications
Laura J. Moore, M.Ed.
214 Lincoln St., Suite 108
Boston, MA 02134-1346
(617) 254-0118
Designs audiocassette educational and marketing programs. Services include strategic planning, script writing, marketing and distribution, consulting, and project management.

DATABASE SOURCES
Joe Sabah
2512 South University Blvd., #808
Denver, CO 80210
(303) 722-7200
Database of 750 radio talk shows that interview guests by telephone. Comes with a 21-chapter book, *How to Get on Radio Talk Shows All Across America Without Leaving Your Home or Office.*

ENTREPRENEUR AWARD PROGRAMS
Blue Chip Enterprise Award
c/o Mass. Mutual Life Ins.
140 Garden St.
Hartford, CT 06154

Ernst and Young
Entrepreneur of the Year Awards
2121 San Jacinto, Suite 1500
Dallas, TX 75201
(214) 969-9626

Horatio Alger Association of
Distinguished Americans
99 Canal Center Plaza
Alexandria, VA 22314
(703) 684-9444
Fax: (703) 548-3822

(Winners include Mary Kay, Dave Thomas of Wendy's, and Rich DeVos of AmWay.)

Malcolm Baldrige National
Quality Awards
c/o National Institute of Standards and Technology
Administrative Building
Room A-537
Gaithersburg, MD 20899
(301) 975-2036
Awards given annually to small businesses, service companies, or subsidiaries, or manufacturing companies and subsidiaries.

Small Business Administration
10 Causeway St., Room 265
Boston, MA 02222-1093
(617) 565-5572
The U.S. Small Business Administration and Massachusetts Advisory Council annually give awards to the Small Business Person of the Year, an Entrepreneurial Success Award, and a Young Entrepreneur of the Year Award.

Also Look for Contest Listings In:
The Encyclopedia of Associations and *Awards, Honors & Prizes*, both published by Gale Research Co., Book Tower, Detroit, MI 48226.

EXPERT LISTINGS
You can place advertisements for yourself and your business in these publications, which are circulated to talk-show producers.

Creative Broadcast
Success Journal Corporation
2516 Waukegan Rd., Suite 301
Glenview, IL 60025
Contact: Chris Whitting, (847) 583-9000

Radio-TV Interview Report
Bradley Communications Corp.
135 East Plumstead Ave.
Landsdowne, PA 19050
(610) 259-1070
Published three times per month.

*Yearbook of Experts, Authorities &
Spokespersons*
Broadcast Interview Source
2233 Wisconsin Ave. NW
Washington, D.C. 20007-4104
(800) 995-0311
Published annually.

INFOMERCIAL / TV RETAILING
Home Shopping Network
Merchandising Department
1 HSN Drive
St. Petersburg, FL 33729
(727) 872-1000
Vendor information packets:
(800) 436-1010

National Infomercial Marketing
Association (NIMA)
1225 New York Ave NW
Suite 1200
Washington, DC 20005
(800) 987-6462
(202) 289-6462
Web site: http://www.nima.org

QVC
1365 Enterprise Dr.
West Chester, PA 19380
(610) 701-1000
New product information:
(888) NEW ITEM

MEDIA DIRECTORIES
Broadcasting and Cable Yearbook
R. R. Bowker, New Providence, NJ
$179

*Burrelle's Media Directory:
Radio & Television & Cable*
Burrelle's Information Services
$250

Cable & Station Coverage Atlas
Warren Publishing, Inc.
$375

*Gale Directory of Publications and
Broadcast Media*
Gale Research, Detroit, MI
$395

*Plunkett's Entertainment and Media
Industry Almanac: The Complete
Guide to America's Publishing,
Broadcasting and Entertainment
Business*
Plunkett Research,
$149.99

PRESENTATION MATERIAL
PRODUCTIONS
Ad Graphics
5829 South 81st East Place
Tulsa, OK 74145
(918) 252-1103
Book design, layout, and other
graphics-related work.

Presentation Graphics
1165 Massachusetts Ave.
Arlington, MA 02476
(781) 646-9840
In-house lab/film processing/
large-format poster printing/multi-
media/CD writing

PROGRAM SYNDICATION
Chris Whitting, (847) 583-9000
Currently has a syndicated program
on more than two hundred radio stations. Whitting has been a program
director, producer, and talent for such
stations as WCBS in New York and
KDKA in Pittsburgh.

PUBLISHING RESOURCES
About Books
Box 1500-B
425 Cedar St.
Buena Vista, CO 81211-1500
(800) 548-1876
(719) 395-2459
Tom and Marilyn Ross
About Books can help with all aspects
of publishing a book: project analysis,
writing and editing, book design, production, and marketing. Call for a
brochure.

*Freelance Writing for Magazines and
Newspapers: Breaking In Without
Selling Out*, HarperCollins

How to Write Irresistible Query Letters
by Lisa Collier Cool
Writer's Digest Books, 1987
(800) 289-0963
$11.99

Self-Publishing Manual
By Dan Poynter
Para Publishing
P.O. Box 8206
Santa Barbara, CA 93118
(805) 968-7277
Considered the Bible of
self-publishing advice.

Writer's Market
Writer's Digest Books
(800) 289-0963
Updated annually.
$27.99, $49.99 with CD

SPEAKING ORGANIZATIONS
National Speakers Association
1500 South Priest Dr.
Tempe, AZ 85281
(602) 968-2552
Fax: (602) 968-0911

Toastmasters
P.O. Box 9052
Mission Viejo, CA 92690-9052
(949) 858-TALK/858-8255
Call (800) 947-3744 to leave a
message and be referred to a
Toastmasters club in your area.
Fax: (949) 858-1207

WEB SITES
*StrikingItRich.com: Profiles of 23
Incredibly Successful Websites You've
Probably Never Heard Of*
by Jaclyn Easton
McGraw-Hill; 1988
$14.95

WRITING ORGANIZATIONS
American Society of Journalists and
Authors, Inc.
Dial-A-Writer
1501 Broadway, Suite 302
New York, NY 10036
(212) 398-1934
Fax: (212) 768-7414

National Writers Union
National Office (13 local chapters)
113 University Place, 6th floor
New York, NY 10003
(212) 254-0279

MADCAP MARKETING: THE POWER OF PIZZAZZ

ElEVeN

BE ORIGINAL—EVEN WHEN YOU DON'T HAVE A BUCK

I was applying for a job at a jeans company, so I wrote my resume on a piece of denim. I was hired on the spot.
PRODUCT-DEVELOPMENT COORDINATOR
COSMOPOLITAN, OCTOBER 1997

1. Be aggressive.
2. Use humor.
3. Have chutzpah.

In today's business world, even if you're the best, you've got to keep reminding your customers. Sometimes it means doing something unusual to attract attention, to make sure that clients and customers remember you. You need pizzazz. You need Madcap Marketing. Once you have a quality product or service, there's nothing wrong with doing something wacky, wild, or crazy to get attention. Sometimes it's exactly what it takes to get noticed.

MADCAP MARKETING:

- Gets you noticed, especially when the competition is fierce
- Entices customers to take a closer look at your products and services

- Presents you as clever—and people like doing business with someone resourceful and inventive

1. BE AGGRESSIVE.

If money is no object, it's never a problem to attract attention. You can simply hire a public-relations person who can implement a wealth of effective strategies. But some of the most ingenious Madcap Marketing has come from entrepreneurs who didn't have a dime to spare. Necessity is the mother of invention, and it holds true when it comes to marketing.

Barry Potekin, owner of the Chicago fast-food franchise Gold Coast Dogs, had no money for advertising and publicity when he opened his business back in 1985. Then a brilliant idea struck him: Every day he hailed a cab, went around the block a few times, and wound up back at the restaurant; during that time Potekin talked the driver's ears off about Gold Coast Dogs. When they arrived back at the restaurant, Potekin gave each driver a five-dollar tip to spend on a meal at Gold Coast Dogs. Today, taxis are parked three-deep outside the restaurants, while the cabbies have the answer for every out-of-towner who asks, "Where's a good place to go for lunch around here?"

Potekin's advice is simple: "Whatever you do in life, your job is to become a diamond in a sea of marbles.... In America you can make money out of thin air, if you're clever." Potekin also has a memorable analogy that points out the advantages of being a leader. In his view it's just like being the lead dog pulling a sled; if you're not in front, "you'll spend the entire day looking at someone's behind," he quips.

Steve Latour desperately wanted a national flower company to sell his handmade leis on the East Coast. But *how* was the million-dollar question. So Latour called 1-800-FLOWERS daily, asked if they carried leis, and when told no, advised his listener that they should carry them, especially on the East Coast. His *modus operandi* was to create a false demand for his flowers, with the hope that his company would get a chance. Thanks to other tactics as well, Latour got his chance. On the day when corporate executives were to make their decision about carrying Latour's leis, Latour decided to do something outrageous. He spent $155 and arranged for a man in a gorilla suit, wearing a white tuxedo and top hat, to deliver ten Hawaiian-style pizzas to the company's Long Island headquarters. It worked. "I wanted to impress these people," says Latour. "I asked myself, 'What would be wacky and outrageous and impress 1-800-FLOWERS?'"

Tom First and Tom Scott, owners of Nantucket Nectars in Boston, also utilized an unusual approach from 1993 through 1995. After they realized that politicians were allowed to hang election banners on highway overpasses, they hung their own signs that read, "Tom and Tom for U.S. Senate," and which also included, of course, the words "Nantucket Nectars." They also sent promoters across the country in purple Winnebagos, giving out free samples. All of their marketing efforts paid off; today Nantucket Nectars has established markets in more than thirty states plus Canada, Europe, Korea, and South and Central America.

HANG YOUR NAME OUT THERE.

Stonyfield Farm, the Boston based purveyor of all-natural yogurt, doesn't use paid advertising. Instead, entrepreneur Gary Hirshberg relies on his natural ability to identify marketing opportunities in the most unusual places. Once, when a Boston radio-show host claimed that he would rather eat camel manure than natural foods, Hirshberg showed up at the station, the very next day, with a gallon of frozen camel manure and some yogurt. He gained immediate attention and an endorsement for Stonyfield. Another time, his employees handed out free yogurt to visitors outside the *Today* show at New York's Rockefeller Center, which also resulted in national exposure. At other times, the company sends out "Moosletters" that explain the firm and its mission, plus five coupons to stimulate buying. It's even gone so far as to create an "Adopt-a-Cow" that generated huge visibility for Stonyfield.[1]

---

[1] *What's Luck Got to Do with It?*, John Wiley & Sons, Inc., 1997, Chap. 8.

2. USE HUMOR.

Jill Smith was once known to hundreds of people as the "Bean Queen" (and it even said so on her business card). Smith and her husband, Doug, founded Buckeye Beans of Spokane, Washington. They won numerous awards and in 1996 were named the SBA's Small Business Persons of the Year for their state. When the Smiths started their business, they launched a newsletter that became legendary due to their "Weird Recipe of the Month," which was a spoof. The recipes included Bean Kebobs, and even summer Bean-cicles (blenderized beans frozen into Dixie cups). "Nobody read the newsletters," says Jill. "But everyone read the Weird Recipe of the Month. Six or seven years later, people still called and asked us for the Weird Recipe of the Month."

Smith says that humor was a big part of the business. They included "Wacky Wednesdays" when employees took silly breaks instead of coffee breaks. The day also included a company-bought lunch for all employees, which was headed by Doug; irreverently named "Dining with Dougie," it was a nonthreatening environment in which each manager gave a three-minute talk about his or her department. "You didn't exist here if you didn't have a sense of humor," says Jill with a laugh.

At the end of each year, you surely turn on the TV to hear about this year's "worst-dressed list." The list was created by a Mr. Blackwell—whose claim to fame is, well, his "worst-dressed list." We don't know if Mr. Blackwell ever actually designed anything—but his laughable list gets mountains of media attention for him annually!

Layla, a restaurant that opened in New York in November 1995, devised a humorous method to market its Middle Eastern food and its unconventional wines to customers. The reason? Many people are tentative about ordering a bottle of wine with their baba gannoujh. But the music and belly dancing inspired the owners to create a witty wine list. Categories include "What to drink when lost in the desert?" and "Which wine will impress your boss?" So far, the plan has worked faster than you can say "hummus."[2] The owners have discovered that when patrons feel more at ease, and are less intimidated and more comfortable with the wine list, they are more apt to order a bottle.

---

[2] *Food Arts,* March 1996, p. 22.

⇥ *Layla Wine List* ⇤

Sparkling

What do They Drink in the French Foreign Legion?

Zardetto Prosecco N.V., Italy	32.
Nicolas Feuillatte Brut Premier Cru, Champagne	48.
Pacific Echo Brut Rose by Sharffenberger, Mendocino County	50.
Moët Chandon Brut Imperial N.V., Champagne	58.
'J' by Jordan 1994, Sonoma	60.
Veuve Clicquot Brut N.V., Champagne demi 38. /	75.
Veuve Clicquot Carte D'Or 1990, Champagne	95.
Dom Perignon 1990, Champagne	175.
La Grande Dame 1989, Champagne	195.

Rosè

What to Drink with Baba Gannoujh and a Mess of Other Mezze?

Domaine De Sahari Vin Gris 1996, Guerrouane Morocco	22.
Regaliali Rosato 1996, Sicilia	23.
McDowell Valley Grenache Rose 1996, Mendocino County	24.

White

Why is This Wine Different From all Other Wines?

Retsina Sitia N.V., Greece	18.

What were Cleopatra's Favorites?

Argiolas Vermentino di Sardegna 1996, Sardegna	25.
Dr. Konstantin Frank Johannisberg Riesling 1997, New York	27.
Girard Chenin Blanc 1996, 'Old Vine', Napa Valley	29.
Trimbach Pinot Gris 1995, Alsace	31.
Fillaboa Albarino 1996, Rias Baixas, Spain	33.
Livio Felluga Pinot Grigio 1997, Collio	35.
Blanck Pinot Auxeroiss 1997, 'Vieilles Vignes', Alsace	36.
Chateau Musar 1994, Lebanon	37.

What to Drink When Lost in the Desert?

Yarden Sauvignon Blanc 1995, Galil, Israel	22.
Coppola *presents* Bianco 1997, California	24.
Les Comtes de Jonqueyres Blanc 1995, Bordeaux	26.
Honig Sauvignon Blanc 1997, Napa Valley	27.
King Estate Pinot Gris 1997, Oregon	29.
Groth Sauvignon Blanc 1997, Napa Valley	32.
Kent Rasmussen Sauvignon Blanc 1996, Napa Valley	36.
Cakebread Cellars Sauvignon Blanc 1997, Napa Valley	37.
Sancerre Chavignol 1997, Bailly-Reverdy, Loire	39.

What Wines did Noah Bring on the Ark?

Chablis~Sécher Premier Cru 1996, Joseph Drouhin, Burgundy	half	24.
Zaca Mesa Chardonnay 1997, Santa Barbara County		30.
Pouilly Fuisse 1997 Vincent, Burgundy		34.
Calera Chardonnay 1997, Central Coast		35.
Chateau Routas Coquelicot 1996, France		36.
Bacchus Reserve Chardonnay 1997 'Barrel Fermented', Napa		39.
Iron Horse Chardonnay 1997, Green Valley, Sonoma		45.
Chalk Hill Chardonnay 1996, 'Estate Bottled', Sonoma County		55.
ZD Chardonnay 1996, California		60.
Puligny Montrachet 1996, Jadot, Burgundy		78.
Kistler Chardonnay 1996, 'Sonoma Coast', Sonoma		79.
Peter Michael 'Belle Cote' 1996, Knights Valley		85.

3. HAVE CHUTZPAH.

The famous author Clare Booth Luce, when she realized that she wanted to work for Condé Nast Publications in 1929, showed the nerve that got her where she wanted to be. Luce first interviewed with publisher Condé Nast, then with *Vogue* editor Edna Woolman Chase. When neither one hired her, Luce simply showed up at *Vogue* one day, convinced an assistant she was an employee, and apparently sat at an empty desk and started working. Apparently, both Nast and Chase thought that the other one had hired Luce! Luce created a job for herself, and later went on to write the famous play, *The Women*.[3]

A Boston interior designer, who wishes to remain anonymous, employed a similar tactic when pitching a new account. Eager to impress a potential client who was to attend a meeting in his office, the newly launched designer realized that his business might not seem big—or busy—enough. To make a better impression, the designer hired, just for that day, two "assistants"; not only did they make the staff seem larger, but their mission was to continually call the office from newly installed phone lines *within* the office. The phones continually rang off the hook, and the assistants kept interrupting the meeting, saying that there was an important decision to be made. The upshot? The designer got the account!

HOW CAN YOU BE A MADCAP MARKETER?

First, brainstorm with your friends, family, customers, and colleagues. Perhaps you could host an informal "pizza night" and invite everyone over, with the goal of helping you come up with new strategies.

Second, visit joke shops, toy stores, card shops, party-planning stores and paper-goods stores, where a product might spark an idea or a promotional tie-in (see p. 139 for ideas). Rick McKenna, a public-relations executive in Concord, Massachusetts, achieved great success with the scores of hollow plastic fish that he

---

[3] *Vanity Fair*, May 1997, p. 173.

purchased for one dollar each at Buck-A-Book. His goal was to get the attention of magazine editors. So, he bought the rubber fish and mailed them to magazine editors, with the message "Expect a flood of information" on the outside of the envelopes. Then he put his press kits in the hollow plastic fish and shipped them out. "Editors called me to get a second fish for their kids," says McKenna with a laugh. "We got a really good response."

Third, read trade publications outside of your business to see if they generate any new ideas or unusual angles. For example, a quick read of *Food Arts* or *Pastry Art & Design* might percolate some innovations that could be translated to your business or industry, even if you are a super successful widget maker. Why not bake small individual cakes shaped like you-know-whats, to hand out to customers?

Fourth, create your own personal trademark—as did the late Minnie Pearl with her hat-with-the-price-tag. Where would Madonna be without her (depending on the month in which she reinvents herself) fingerless gloves, Jean-Paul Gaultier bra, Gucci hiphugger pants, or Hindu garb?

Remember Patricia Fripp, the speaker who wears funny hats? Like Fripp, professional speaker Larry Winget is known for the more than thirty pairs of interesting eyeglasses that he wears when speaking. Even if his audience forgets his name, they remember him as "the guy with the glasses."

In Boston, top party-planner Marilyn Riseman can stop traffic with her dramatic Kabuki-like makeup, which she collaborated on with makeup artist David Nicholas. Riseman always wears her black hair in a sleek bob style, and wears jet-black eye shadow that rims her eyes. Once you see her, you don't forget her, and in Riseman's business—as in yours—that's the name of the game!

What it all boils down to is having a gimmick. Chapter 12 discusses how to get your own gimmick, and shows you how to create a niche, make your business memorable, and be provocative. Tallyho!

TwelVe

GET A GIMMICK

Most ideas are not unusual, but the experience of having ideas is unusual.
THE TOASTMASTER'S TREASURE CHEST, ©1979, P. 269.

1. Create your niche.
2. Make yourself memorable.
3. Be provocative.

There's a scene in the musical *Gypsy* that sums up this chapter. In a burlesque-house dressing room, three strippers advise a young Gypsy Rose Lee about their act. One, dressed as a Roman gladiator and brandishing a trumpet, says, "What you need to have is an idea that makes your strip special." The second stripper adds ballet to her bumps-and-grinds, while the third, outfitted in a costume adorned with electric light bulbs, suggests, "If you want to make it, twinkle while you shake it." All three tell Gypsy, "You've got to get a gimmick, if you want to get ahead."

So if you want to be electrifying—with a minimum of trying—you must be an Original Marketeer and do things that are provocative...zany...innovative...and attention-getting. Why not break some of the rules? The ultimate goal of Madcap Marketing is to bring business your way by creating and establishing unique memorable experiences. How do you want to be remembered?

1. CREATE YOUR NICHE.

Sometimes the best marketing tools are found where you least expect them. When Warren Avis was an Air Force captain during World War II, he made a discovery that he refers to as one of his "supreme mountaintop achievements." The concept? Avis Airlines Rent-A-Car. During the war Avis traveled everywhere, but no destination offered decent ground transportation. He even took to carrying his motorcycle in the bomb bays of his plane so he could travel after landing.

In 1946 and 1947, you couldn't rent an automobile in airports. Not even Hertz, which at that time had offices in cities across the United States. In fact, explains Avis in his book, *Take a Chance to Be First,* rent-a-car offices were frequently located in back-alley garages, where you could rent an old jalopy. Renting a car, back then, was a long, laborious process. So, expanding on the rent-a-car idea, Avis put car rentals into major airports and in highly visible areas of cities all over the world. He pioneered credit-card rentals, the use of new cars, and the hiring of women to work the counters. Within seven years, the company had become the world's second-largest international rent-a-car system. Because Avis didn't have deep pockets of cash to market and promote his business, he used his creativity. He convinced the airlines to insert Avis pamphlets in every plane's seat pockets, so the captive audience of travelers could learn about this new concept; the Avis stuffer, in effect, was a forerunner of today's in-flight magazines. This one simple step educated thousands of travelers about this new car-rental concept.

Avis, who started the business in his twenties, sold it in his thirties—for several million dollars.

Patch Products, inventors of the successful TriBond game, convinced fourteen Rocky Rococo pizzerias in the Madison, Wisconsin, area, to put sample TriBond clue cards on their tables, so that patrons could play the game while dining. They also enticed 250 disc jockeys nationwide to read

Points to remember:

- Be a pioneer.
- Think big.
- Creatively inform your prospects.

TriBond clues on the air. The ploys paid off; after these creative marketing tactics, Patch sold 250,000 copies of TriBond. Today, sales have topped 1.5 million and the product line has been extended to include four versions including a game for kids, another for preschoolers, and even a Bible TriBond.

Tova Borgnine created her own gimmick too. She is a millionaire many times over, thanks to smart marketing of her Tova Corporation beauty products. Her success began right at the starting gate, when she sold her "facelift in a jar" cactine mask in an unusual way: through mail-order advertising in city newspapers. "It went totally against traditional marketing," says Borgnine. "But if I had done it traditionally, and gone against brands sold typically in department stores, I couldn't have survived."

That move had yet another advantage: "Mail order is a cash business, and it helped me establish lines of credit," says the brainy beauty.

The result is that Borgnine eventually built a successful business that now is in its ninth successful year of being sold on QVC. In that time, she has sold more than 1 million bottles of her fragrances, while the company has experienced double-digit growth annually for the past three years. Her advice? "Look at what someone's *not* doing, and find that niche…. I didn't follow anyone else's lead."

Tessa Greenspan also followed that road. When she took over ownership of the nearly bankrupt Sappington Farmers Market in St. Louis, Missouri, she knew that she needed more than quality products and great values to compete with supermarket giants. She knew that it would take ongoing promotions to heighten the market's visibility and attract new customers. Her gimmick? She installed an electric train that ran continuously on an elevated track in the store's interior. The train, complete with suspension bridges and whistle, bears mini-billboards announcing the daily specials, and captured the imagination of young and old customers alike. Later, Greenspan added realistic villages and rural scenes. Today, revenues have more than exceeded Greenspan's projections and she has opened a second Sappington Farmers Market after outgrowing the first store. She also created the largest ethnic food department in the area, and hired a German "meat meister" to create authentic foods not normally available in her area.

BE OVER-THE-TOP

We could all learn a thing or two from Yolanda Cellucci, a well-known Boston personality who owns an eponymous salon and designer boutique in the neighboring suburb of Waltham, Massachusetts. (It's simply known as "Yolanda," and the one-name title, like "Cher" or "Madonna," is another smart marketing technique.) From the start, Cellucci knew she had to do *something* to get people to Waltham. "So I started doing outrageous, overglamorous things to attract people," she says. Yolanda's store carried feathered, fur-trimmed designs that were "very Hollywood and Las Vegas," she says. Celebrities, pageant contestants, and showgirls all became regular customers. But since no one wears fur-trimmed dresses all the time, Cellucci also made a point to sell "lots of basic clothes too." After business picked up, she traded her white Pontiac Grand Prix for two Excalibur cars; one was a coupe, which she used herself. The other was a limousine that bears her name on its door. "It was an advertising card," says Cellucci. "It became my signature. You couldn't help but look at it. It was the way to go." When the bank told her she was crazy to take out a $12,000 loan for the limousine, she told them her marketing brainstorm: She would rent it to brides, as well as people celebrating birthdays and anniversaries. "It makes money and it advertises me all day long," she says. Even better, "you couldn't buy a billboard for less than twelve thousand dollars a year—and the car advertises me wherever it goes....The Excaliburs are my marketing tools, and part of my success," she adds.

2. MAKE YOURSELF MEMORABLE.

On the West Coast, Jack Roberts of Lynnwood, Washington, also believes in featuring himself in his marketing efforts. Owner of a chain of appliance stores, Roberts has increased his sales fivefold over the past decade by starring in several zany television commercials. The wilder your ads are, the better you can differentiate yourself from the competition, Roberts believes. Turn on the tube and you might see Roberts bisecting a television with a chain saw to illustrate that he was cutting prices. Or, he might outfit his sales help as overpriced appliances and chase them away. Roberts decided against a staid approach to his advertising, as he believed that Madison Avenue would emphasize the similarities, not the differences, between his company and the competition.

"I can purchase standardized advertisements (canned, non-original spots) from my professional organization, but never have because I want to be known for being unique," says Roberts. "I can't grab the attention of viewers when I look like everybody else," he says.

Roberts's commercials have turned him into something of a local celebrity. Twice he has been invited to play a game of basketball against the Globetrotters before an audience of more than thirteen thousand in the Tacomadome. He's been written up in local Seattle newspapers, and even featured on *48 Hours*.

Cerie Segal, a travel journalist heard on the ABC Radio Networks and beyond, also knows all about making herself memorable. Four years ago, when the Plano, Texas–based broadcaster wanted to move her show to a bigger station, she found the perfect method: ten-dollar inflatable globe-printed beachballs. Segal boxed her demo tape with an inflated globe, and a message that said, "Let me bring the world to your listeners." Then she had each package hand-delivered to several radio stations. "It led to my current on-air job," says Segal. The ploy obviously made an impression. "It not only got me noticed, but my program director still has that globe in his office!"

Points to remember:

- Grab people's attention.
- Set yourself apart from the competition.
- Put yourself on the line and take a risk.

CREATE CACHET

Entrepreneur Bill Kimpton is chairman of the Kimpton Hotel & Restaurant Group, a chain of boutique hotels that appeal to business travelers. The keys to the hotels' success include affordable rates; freestanding restaurants; and a warm, comfortable atmosphere. All Kimco hotels have a distinct personality and set themselves apart by focusing on one theme. The Juliana Hotel in San Francisco, for example, named all of its rooms after theaters and art galleries. "It was excellent for local business," says Stephen Pinetti, vice president of sales and marketing. "Nobody knew of Bill Kimpton or boutique hotels.... It gave us visibility."

Kimpton's Hotel Vintage Park in Seattle named all of its guest rooms after Washington wineries and vineyards, and even arranges private wine tours and tastings for guests. But the most whimsical is the Hotel Triton in San Francisco; in 1995 it opened a special suite created by the late Grateful Dead founder Jerry Garcia. The one-bedroom suite is adorned in contemporary patterns and colors, in the silk fabrics Garcia used to make his famous neckties. "It attracts Deadheads and others," says Pinetti. "At the Triton, we needed to do a hotel that was different from our other hotels. We said, 'Let's do something avant-garde to attract fashion designers...and we'll promote it to these special industries.'" The response? "Excellent. It's a home run," says Pinetti. "These themed floors and suites definitely run a higher occupancy than the primary hotel rooms and suites. The cachet around the idea is unique," Pinetti adds.

What else is unique? At the Triton, guests are given "Leave Me Alone" placards, instead of the typical "Do Not Disturb" signs. Along with wine and sodas, the honor bars also stock Pez dispensers. And the bathroom amenities include little yellow rubber-duck toys, which are also marketing tools that are given away to clients and journalists.

FIND YOUR COMPANY'S RUBBER DUCKY.

Another atypical Kimpton marketing promotion occurred when the chain encouraged guests to bring their pets to a Kimpton Hotel when traveling. Hotel Monaco, Seattle, even provided willing guests with a pet goldfish during their stay. It sounds ridiculous—but the eccentric idea landed a whimsical feature story in the *Wall Street Journal*.[1]

Last that we heard, Kimpton was thinking of developing "tall people" suites at the Hotel Monaco, Denver, which would feature longer beds and higher shower heads.

---

[1] *HSMAI Marketing Review,* Fall 1998, p. 16.

Bijan, the famous international couturier to the rich and famous, knows how to attract attention to himself—and his two stores—by creating cachet around his business. When the entrepreneur opened his first store he saw customers "By appointment only"—a novel idea in the retailing industry. He still conducts business in the same way. Those three little words have come to set Bijan apart—and heads of state, kings, presidents, and celebrities beat a path to his door, where they get the royal treatment.

SEIZE OPPORTUNITIES TO MAKE AN IMPRESSION

Ginny Rivenburg, owner of a company in Acton, Massachusetts, which creates custom-designed window products, has a unique way to introduce herself at meetings. Rivenburg stands up and says her name, while holding a small "hand sample" shade; while speaking she uses a remote control to make the shade go up and down. "Usually everyone cracks up," says Rivenburg. "It attracts a lot of attention, and it breaks the ice for a lot of people." The result is that the gimmick plants the seed, eventually bringing Rivenburg new business. "The way that I network is unconventional, but it works," she explains.

Points to remember:

- Give your product or service looks and personality.
- Leverage celebrity appeal to your benefit.
- Create cachet around your product or service.

A golfer, Rivenburg also found a way to advertise her business on the golf course. She and her husband are usually paired with strangers, to make a foursome. Rivenburg had golf tees imprinted with "Custom Window Products" and the phone number, which she frequently hands out to her new golf partners. Once, in Florida, she gave the tees away, only to discover that the twosome had children who were moving to the Boston area. Faster than you can say, "Hole in one," the kids called and commissioned Rivenburg to decorate their windows.

Even if you make a mistake, there are innovative ways to impress. Nancy Michaels once sent an invitation that contained a typographical error. After talking to the client and correcting the problem, she sent him a giant eraser with her apologies and a note. It said: "My apologies for the typo; I wish I could have erased it sooner, but I'm working on it as I write."

White-Out could have also done the trick.

ERASE YOUR MISTAKES.

Here are some other memorable marketing ideas from companies that dared to be different.

The Sara Lee Hosiery Company that represents Hanes and L'Eggs once sent out two small red-and-green nylon stockings in its Yuletide cards.

A Boston accounting firm, where one of the partners is Irish, sends out green bagels a week before St. Patrick's Day to the media, and on the holiday to clients and vendors.

A travel agency, which hadn't been in touch with prospective clients for a while, sent a direct-mail piece that resembled a stovetop—a box with a teal-colored square on its top. The message read, "We know your decision on choosing a travel company has been put on the back burner." When the box was opened, another teal square bore the message: "We hope this helps move it to the front." When that square was lifted, clients found a potholder with the travel-agency logo on it.

A dental group wanted to thank patients for their patience with any problems they may have experienced during a time when the practice converted their computer systems. So they sent out a box whose label explained that there were no "half-baked" excuses for the problems. When opened, the package revealed six cookies, and yet another message explaining that the conversion proved to be "one tough cookie."

CREATE A CONVERSATION PIECE.

A Los Angeles–based design firm once sent its clients an award-winning Christmas card filled with numerous gift tags that would definitely be used during the holidays. Now that's a practical gift that everyone can appreciate.

The Kitchen Etc. chain frequently brews coffee and bakes fresh bread in its stores to entice customers to stay put, look at the merchandise, enjoy free samples, and eventually make a purchase. Real-estate agents might do the same. If you're showing a home, have fresh coffee and bread cooking in the kitchen. The aromas will suggest the warm, fuzzy feelings of "home sweet home" and might help you secure the deal.

3. BE PROVOCATIVE.

Violinist Lara St. John found an unusual way to promote herself and her debut album of Bach solo violin works. The cover showed St. John wearing nothing more than her fiddle. Does sex sell? Well, at this writing St. John's CD has sold more than twenty thousand copies.

MORE MEMORABLE MARKETING IDEAS

When sending out a video-demonstration tape or a TV audition tape to clients or the media, package it in an aluminum tray, add utensils, and call it a "TV Dinner."

Send fortune cookies with preprinted messages to new and prospective clients on Chinese New Year's.

Create your own postcard to reach clients.

Buy Tiffany bags and place your information inside; everyone will want to open theirs!

Buy inexpensive wine or champagne bottles and a special "label" or advertisement for your business. (Job-hunters might use a mini-reproduction of their resume.)

Give your clients twelve-month gift subscriptions to industry or business publications, which will remind them of your company year-round.

Send an anniversary card to celebrate when you first worked with a new client. Or send birthday cards on the first and consecutive "birthday" that you sold a product or service such as a computer or car.

Leap to the rescue when your client or colleague runs into a snag. Heroes are not forgotten. Never disparage the competition.

Remember, be consistent and repetitive in your approach. It takes several tries to earn name or brand recognition!

Here are some other ways to pique their curiosity.

After Katrina Garnett founded Crossworlds Software in 1996, she knew she needed something different to attract attention to her company. Why not put a face on her company, to brand it? So she spent nearly $35,000 on her gimmick. Garnett hired celebrity photographer Richard Avedon to shoot a sexy, glamorous picture of her in a Hervé Léger dress. Then she used it in a million-dollar ad campaign that was placed in such non-techy publications as *Vanity Fair, Fortune, W,* and the *New York Times Magazine.* Because the ad so resembled editorial content, it generated huge controversy—and dollars. The untraditional ad led to 1.5 million hits at the company's Web site—just in the first month—and it eventually attracted $40 million in funding from angel investors, and close to $5 million in sales. "Since software is intangible, we decided to put a face on our company," Garnett says. "Customers don't just want to buy software; they buy a relationship. People want to be associated with success, with someone who is confident, powerful, glamorous. Marketing yourself, you realize, is marketing your company."[2]

The advertising exposure also led Garnett to the editorial pages. She was interviewed for the April 1999 issue of *Vogue* magazine, in a feature about "The New Rich."

Good marketing also takes into account what your audience will probably respond to. Rick McKenna, who graduated from Boston University with a degree in Public Relations, used this concept to get his first job. He sent out inexpensive tape recorders that he bought for about fifteen dollars, and paired each one with a six-minute cassette; in the tape he introduced himself and told his listener that he wanted to be different. How did it work? "One hundred percent," says

---

[2] *Success,* Nov. 1998, p. 50.

Points to remember:

- Spend extra money to reach VIPs.
- Search for products that lend themselves to witty messages.
- Rise above the clutter.

McKenna. "For less than twenty dollars I guaranteed myself an interview. Instead of a shotgun blast, it was a rifle shot. Usually the interviewee appreciated my aggressiveness, and said that it was a pleasure to have a different format, instead of the usual resumes or even e-mail."

Another time, McKenna bought cheap telephones that could be pre-programmed with one phone number—that of his client. When the package was opened, the recipient received a phone with a button bearing the message: "Hit here." When it was pushed, the recipient was put in touch with McKenna's client, who made arrangements to be available twenty-four hours a day. "It was expensive, but you got to senior level people and CEOs faster," says McKenna. "Their curiosity factor was piqued. The goal was to rise above the clutter."

BE CREATIVE AND CLEVER

Vidal Herrera, owner of a Los Angeles–based autopsy business, makes his car a moving billboard; it carries the vanity license plate YSPOTUA, which spells "Autopsy" in a rear-view mirror. Not only that, his unorthodox license plate, and the 1-800-AUTOPSY phone number on his van, have been mentioned in the "Perspectives" section of *Newsweek*,[3] earning him even more publicity. "I drive it in traffic on purpose," says Herrera of the marketing ploy he devised in 1994 for his vehicle. Adds his wife, Vicki: "It's the best thing he's ever done."[4]

USE YOUR LICENSE PLATE.

John Sayles and Sheree Clark of Sayles Graphic Design in Des Moines, Iowa, devised a clever strategy for one client. After designing an ad, they had it painted on one bus to promote the client's products and services. Clients, prospects, and friends called them to say that they saw the client's *buses* all over town—the perception being that there was more than one.

[3] July 14, 1997, p. 19.
[4] *People,* Nov. 23, 1998, p. 112.

ThirteeN

DO IT
DIFFERENTLY

> **There are those who would misteach us that to stick in a rut is consistency—and a virtue, and that to climb out of the rut is inconsistency—and a vice.**
> MARK TWAIN, "CONSISTENCY"

1. Brand yourself.
2. Celebrate untraditional holidays.
3. Give unusual gifts and freebies.

She's known as Martha—but when you're a multimillion-dollar conglomerate all in one person, who needs a last name? Martha Stewart started the trend in do-it-yourself luxurious living, which has resulted in her own magazine, books, a television show, and a newspaper column, not to mention a lucrative contract with K-Mart. She created her own distinctive brand—Martha—and so can you. Just do it a little bit differently than everyone else, with Madcap Marketing.

1. BRAND YOURSELF.

Anthony and Lauren Raissen launched their BreathAsure breath freshener at, of all places, the Los Angeles Garlic Festival. "We picked the most offensive odor," says Anthony. They set up a booth and told people to stop by before they left, and take some BreathAsure. Within twenty to thirty minutes, Anthony promised, you'll have fresh, clean breath. A talk-show host who was attending said he thought that claim was impossible. "But he was absolutely amazed," says Anthony, who found himself on the talk show the very next day.

Next, the Raissens began a direct-response advertising campaign; consumers could call an 800 number and purchase the product. Even though grocery stores wouldn't carry the product, the Raissens persuaded health-food stores to stock BreathAsure, which also created product awareness. "We created credibility this way," says Anthony.

The Raissens also made themselves memorable by misspelling the "assure" in BreathAsure. "It makes people think," says Anthony. "People remember it—and you." However, Anthony adds that they didn't purposely set out to misspell the name— they merely ran out of room on the package!

Adds Anthony: "I came to America seven years ago (from South Africa) looking for the American Dream. We believed we would one day find the American Dream." And the Raissens did. Not only is the product flying off the shelves, but Anthony makes it his mission to deal with his audience of consumers. "I work eighteen hours a day, and I pride myself on answering every call that comes to my desk," he says.

Allen-Edmonds, a shoe company based in Port Washington, Wisconsin, has always done an excellent job promoting its footwear—especially in films. The company places a heavy emphasis on creating brand awareness through product placement in movies. For example, Danny DeVito and Jack Nicholson wore Allen-Edmonds shoes in the movie *Hoffa*, Clint

Points to remember:

- What's in a name?
- Dare to be different.
- Create your own credibility.

Eastwood and John Malkovich wore them in *In the Line of Fire*, and Tommy Lee Jones wore them in *The Client*. They've even shod the stars of *Hoodlum*, *There's Something About Mary*, and the blockbuster, *Titanic*. But Allen-Edmonds doesn't just stop at the big screen. Their shoes have been seen on the feet of Tim Allen in *Home Improvement*, Michael Richards on *Seinfeld*, and even Cybill Shephard in her own sitcom. Funnymen Conan O'Brien, Bill Maher, and Craig Kilbourn all wear them too. It prompts lots of media attention. The *Chicago Tribune* and CNN called Allen-Edmonds "the shoemaker to the stars." The *Today* show also shoed into the story. Allen-Edmonds doesn't go through product placement companies to get on the screen, but uses its contacts with Hollywood costumers. "Let's face it, the camera doesn't zoom to a man's shoes," says company president John Stollenwerk. "We get our footwear in the movies because it's fun for all of us and we can gab about it to our dealers and suppliers in our *Shoe Wrap* newsletter. We have an atrium filled with movie posters featuring the roles our shoes play in films. People who tour our corporate headquarters love it, especially the display of shoes worn by U.S. presidents and the ceremonial shoes worn by the athletes at the 1992 Olympics in Barcelona. They get the same thrill my co-workers did when they cut and lasted all those size-eighteens for the Olympics' Dream Team."

Allen-Edmonds continues to read like the "Who's Who" of the "Who's Who." They have shod the feet of U.S. presidents Ronald Reagan, George Bush, and Bill Clinton, as well as Belgium's King Albert II, which prompted an article in the *Washington Post*, stating that Allen-Edmonds was the choice on Capitol Hill. The articles and all those movie roles are touted in the company's promotional materials, further publicizing all the publicity.

Small businesses don't have the financial backing for Hollywood-style product placements—but you might contact local production companies and inquire about their using your product in their next film or video, for a small fee. Or, contact local film and broadcasting schools, and let students know that you will donate some of your products for their student productions. Most costumers, according to Allen-Edmonds, want to work with companies that get their products there on time, even overnight, in order to meet fitting deadlines. Voila! A star—your product—is born!

TELL THE WORLD ABOUT THE CELEBRITIES WHO USE YOUR PRODUCT OR SERVICE.

NIX THE BORING NAMETAG!

Boston-based writer Marcia Yudkin has found a clever way to make herself memorable, and also sell copies of her book, *Six Steps to Free Publicity*, with a minimum of effort. Yudkin took her book's cover, had it reduced and laminated, and now wears it as a nametag at all business and networking meetings, and at trade shows. "It starts a conversation," says Yudkin. "People say, 'Oh, what's that?. . . Tell me about your book.'" Yudkin says that the nametag cost her only $2.50, but reaps a wealth of sales. "I sell three or four books by the end of each meeting," she says.

Graphic designer Linda Patterson of Needham, Massachusetts, also has an unusual nametag. She took two of the brochure covers she designed, shrunk them into thumbnail-sized miniatures, and mounted them on her nametag. "You can even open the top one," she says. The effect? "People walk up to me and say, 'How cute.' It says that this person has creative ideas—and that's what I'm selling. They remember me as the lady with the unique nametag."

WEAR YOUR OWN SPECIAL, PERSONALIZED, DIFFERENT-LOOKING NAMETAG.

2. CELEBRATE UNTRADITIONAL HOLIDAYS.

Why bother with the December holidays, when everyone is bombarded with mail? Another way to practice Madcap Marketing is to celebrate unconventional holidays appropriate to your business. Michaels's company, ImpressionImpact

Productions, celebrates Chinese New Year's; these slower times of the year allow more time for mailings to the media, customers, and prospective clients, and don't compete with the typical Christmas rush. As a result, Michaels's mailings tend to be remembered.

Leon & Company, an award-winning hair salon in Belmont, Massachusetts, recently reaped great success with its proclamation of the third week in March as "Good Hair Week in Massachusetts." To attract new clients, the salon tied in with Wella Corporation and offered free samples worth twenty-five dollars to each new customer. The week-long event also included free Polaroids to all customers (who had a new haircut or color), free blow-dry consultations, a wealth of valuable prizes including dinner-for-two with limousine transportation, wardrobe consultations and makeovers, and other image-related gifts. A portion of the proceeds was also donated to charity. The unusual event generated positive press in the *Boston Business Journal*, the front page of the *Belmont Citizen-Herald*, as well as coverage on radio and over the Internet.

Safar Coiffure, one of Boston's leading hair salons, also hit the mark when its French owner decided to capitalize on July 14th—Bastille Day. He ran a special promotion offering free French manicures to everyone who had their hair done that day, and several local newspapers picked up the story.

WHEN IN FRANCE . . .

CREATE YOUR OWN HOLIDAY

Why not just make up your own marketing holiday? Just submit your application to *Chase's Calendar of Events*. It's a day-by-day directory of nationwide festivals, celebrity birthdays, historical anniversaries, culinary celebrations, entertainment awards, astronomical phenomena, presidential proclamations, and more. The 1995 guide, for example, included "National Clean Out Your Refrigerator Day" (November 15) sponsored by Whirlpool Corporation, a sweet-corn festival sponsored by the Sun Prairie,

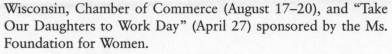
Wisconsin, Chamber of Commerce (August 17–20), and "Take Our Daughters to Work Day" (April 27) sponsored by the Ms. Foundation for Women.

In 1995, Michaels created MarketAbility Month in January, which was designed to heighten awareness of the importance of self-marketing. As a result, Michaels found herself on the *Weekend Today* show in New York!

3. GIVE UNUSUAL GIFTS AND FREEBIES.

Giving unique gifts to your clients is yet another way to set yourself apart. For example, if one of your clients lands in the hospital, why send predictable gifts like flowers or a fruit basket? A Madcap Marketer would send a basket filled with herbal tea, magazines, a cooling eye mask, and an old movie on video. Or, if the patient was a real movie buff, you could send several old movies, popcorn, and a box of Raisinets, plus two tickets to the cinema to be used after recovery. Bear in mind the specific interests of your customers and clients; specialty and gift shops offer unusual items geared to doctors, attorneys, golf and cooking enthusiasts, you name it. If you visit a client when he's having a rough day, send a giant, mammoth-sized aspirin (found in specialty stores—see the end of this chapter) to humorously relieve his headache. A carefully chosen gift that shows extra thought goes a long way. For more excellent, unusual gifts, see the book *It's Just What I've Always Wanted* by Chiquita Woodard (Hyperion, $11.95).

PUT A GREAT DEAL OF THOUGHT INTO YOUR GIFTS; FORGET THE FLOWERS.

Being generous with your thank yous and referrals is an overlooked—but very important way to set yourself apart. It sounds obvious, but too many people fail to recognize this simple tactic. Always send thank-you notes when someone has helped you; handwritten notes are often appropriate when you know the person. The important thing is to do it! Putting two people together with referrals is another way to make yourself invaluable to customers and clients.

GIVE AWAY FREEBIES

Your mother told you it was better to give than to receive. And she was right!

The mother-of-all-marketing is probably Estee Lauder. Mrs. Lauder initially ran her business from her kitchen; she originally set herself apart by selling her homemade creams to prestigious department stores whereas her competitors, such as Helena Rubenstein, sold their products to pharmacies. Mrs. Lauder also had the brainstorm of offering a free gift with a cosmetics purchase; today the gift-with-purchase—"gwp"—is ubiquitous in the beauty industry. Not only do most of the other cosmetics companies follow her example, but today, according to the *Wall Street Journal*, Estee Lauder and its other lines, including Clinique and Prescriptives, pull in thirty-nine cents of every dollar spent on U.S. department-store cosmetics.[1]

Richard Evans, the author of the best-seller *The Christmas Box*, found that giving away free copies of his book led to overwhelming success. Evans admits that when he self-published his book, "We didn't have the money to compete, and I didn't know how to do it." But the advertising executive soon learned that "if people read the book, they would also buy extra copies for friends."

After Evans gave away twenty copies for Christmas he made an amazing discovery: "People called me up saying that they had had an emotional experience reading the book. In four weeks those books had been read one hundred sixty times....Obviously we had the beginning of a trend here."

He soon self-published nine thousand more copies which immediately sold out, aided by counter displays and posters that

---

[1] Nov. 8, 1995, p. A10.

he designed. Then he printed ten thousand more, which also sold out. Then Evans got a brainstorm; he asked seven thousand radio stations to give away copies of the book for their Yuletide promotions, and asked them to say, "If you only read one book this Christmas, make it this one." Evans got more than five hundred responses. "Radio stations ate it up," he says. "Even some of the DJs got emotional in their endorsements."

Eventually Simon & Schuster spent more than $4 million for the hardcover rights to *The Christmas Box,* which found its way onto the *New York Times* bestseller list.

Evans used savvy marketing, but really capitalized on a long-known truth: most people like to get something for nothing. Let's face it, even wealthy party-goers clamor for the goodie bags that are frequently given away at posh events.

Your customers aren't any different; that's why you should follow Evans's example and also offer freebies. Giving away freebies creates a positive experience in the mind of the potential customers, thus making your business memorable. Freebies bearing your business name and address also serve as a constant reminder. When potential customers see, feel, taste, touch, and hear your product, it may lead to future sales. The makers of Smartfood popcorn gave away loads of free samples in the company's infancy; eventually the business grew so big that Frito-Lay came knocking at their door and bought them out. Eileen Spitalny, owner of Fairytale Brownies in Scottsdale, Arizona, attributes her company's great success to freebies. "By sending sample brownies and a press release, we have gotten continuous national exposure, which helps us spread the word. It's a great marketing tool for us, when our budget is very limited."

In 1998, the Cape Cod Potato Chip company in Hyannis, Massachusetts, launched a "Thanks for Nothing" promotion, to tie in with the final episode of *Seinfeld*—the show about "nothing." They simply asked customers to send in nothing— nothing but their name and address—to receive a free bag of chips.

What can you give away? The easiest thing is to offer free sample sizes of your product. It's worked well for businesses in the food, beverage, and beauty industry, so why not yours?

Whatever you do, make sure that the free items pertain to your business. Ice-cream shop owners might print "good for one free cone" on the back of their business cards. A hair salon could give away styling brushes, or samples of shampoo. A travel agency might pass out keychains, umbrellas, or Swiss Army knives. A wake-up service could send out packets of coffee.

Or consider giving away useful freebie items bearing your name—called "premiums." Your business name, address, and phone number, and even a special message, can be prominently displayed on such items as notepads, pens, notebooks, magnets, calendars, T-shirts, visors, sunglasses, you name it.

Some companies even offer items that are as creative as they are promotional (see p. 140). The specialty company Manufacturer's Direct, for example, offers inexpensive rubber thongs that can bear a corporate name or logo on their soles, so that the name of the business gets imprinted in the sand with each footstep. A nifty idea for a beachfront inn, hotel, or restaurant, right?

GREAT REASONS FOR GIVEAWAYS

Grand openings	Thank-you gifts any time of year
Anniversary celebrations	Seasonal
New branch opening	Trade shows
Holiday gifts	New product launch

UNUSUAL PREMIUM GIFTS WITH YOUR LOGO OR MESSAGE

Bottled water	Musical business cards
Gourmet coffee	Jugs and coolers
Sunblock	Sunglasses
Chocolate champagne bottle	Old-fashioned pretzels
Rubber thongs with your message on the bottom	Fortune cookies

David Gaw of Nashville, Tennessee, also found great success with freebies. His company developed a special cream for temporary relief of pain from arthritis, sore muscles, and backache; its special ingredient is a pepper extract. Gaw's company, DAPAT Pharmaceuticals, planned to break even by selling its

"Dr.'s Cream," and then purchase advertising. But sales remained stagnant. "We had to differentiate ourselves someway," says Gaw's son, Jeff. David found the answer in a small bag of peanuts that a flight attendant distributed to him one day while traveling. David figured that if he gave away samples, customers might eventually buy. He found a packager who put one-tenth-ounce samples in packets, at a cost of fourteen cents each. Each DAPAT account received twenty-five free sample packets, which they handed out to customers. "No competitors were giving out samples," Jeff says. "We succeeded in differentiating ourselves while adding to our profit margin."

The more samples that were given out, the more pharmacies became familiar with the product. As a result, they began recommending Dr.'s Cream. In the first three months after the introduction of samples, sales doubled. Pharmacies that ordered twelve or more jars received twenty-five additional samples.

The sample system began in Fall 1991. Sales at the end of the year were $93,000. The next year they jumped to $369,000. By 1993 they rose to $862,000. By 1994 sales reached $1.3 million. With the added revenues, the company increased its television and advertising budgets, and the cream is now available in almost every major drugstore in Tennessee as well as in Walgreen's, Wal-Mart, and other chains nationwide. The company also received a 1995 Blue Chip Enterprise Initiative Award sponsored by *Nation's Business* magazine, Connecticut Mutual Life Insurance Company, and the U.S. Chamber of Commerce.[2]

Points to remember:

• Give and get.
• Use common sense.
• Success breeds more success.

We hope that this chapter has provided you with a wealth of wacky, effective ideas to pack some punch—and pizzazz—into your marketing efforts. Now, though, you're probably ready to spread around some of your success by strategically aligning yourself, and your business, with civic causes. The next chapter on Civic Marketing will show you how to do just that, and also reap the rewards deserved from such civic-minded endeavors.

[2] *Insights and Inspiration: How Businesses Succeed, The 1995 Blue Chip Enterprise Initiative,* published by Connecticut Mutual Life Insurance Company, p. 48.

PART FOUR RESOURCES:

ADVERTISING SPECIALTY COMPANIES

Ha-Lo Advertising Specialties
5980 W. Touhy Ave.
Niles, IL 60714
(800) 676-HALO (4256)
(708) 647-4902
Fax: (708) 647-4902

Manufacturer's Direct
6B Strawberry Hill
P.O. Box 2345
Acton, MA 01720
(978) 263-7788
Fax: (978) 263-3535

Premiums "R" Us
220 Boylston St.
Chestnut Hill, MA 02467
(800) 895-2020
Fax: (617) 558-2841

Promotional Products
Association, International
3125 Skyway Circle North
Irving, TX 75038-3526
Call (972) 252-0404 for a directory
(888) 492-6891 (membership number)
listing distributors in your area.

BOOKS

Big Marketing Ideas for Small Service Businesses by Tom and Marilyn Ross. Dow Jones-Irwin, $24.95.

Chase's Calendar of Events
NTC/Contemporary Publishing
4255 W. Touhy Ave.
Lincolnwood, IL 60646-1975
(847) 679-5500
Fax: (847) 679-6388

Available at the library or any super bookstore, $47.95. Deadline for submissions is May 15. Submit exact name of event; exact inclusive dates for the following year; location (site, city, and state); brief description of the event; formula (if used to set date each year on an annual basis, or the first Saturday in October, etc.); name, title, and address of person to be listed; phone number; sponsor (if any); name of contact person with signature; number of people attending; calendar with circled dates.

It's Just What I've Always Wanted by Chiquita Woodard. Hyperion, $11.95. Filled with a wealth of gift ideas for all people, occasions, and price ranges.

VENDORS

Barrels of Fun!
385 Pleasant St.
Fall River, MA 02721
(800) 5-FOR-FUN
Fax: (508) 646-9735
E-mail: barrels@shore.net
Internet:
http://www.barelsoffun.com/gifts
Barrels filled with candies, toys, and trinkets relevant to your holiday and special occasions for clients, prospects, employees, etc.

Brenner's Super Discount Party Supply
31 Osprey Rd.
Saugus, MA 01906
(781) 231-0555
Gifts, seasonal items, and party supplies too numerous to mention, at low prices. A great place to gather ideas. Don't forget to "steal" a few ideas from the bridal business!

Cookies by Miss Jackie
360 Salem St.
Malden, MA 02148
(781) 322-3792
Fax: (781) 397-9972
A specialty bakery that custom designs cookie baskets and centerpieces. Delivery is available in the Boston area and shipping is nationwide. Seasonal, wedding, shower, baby shower, and holiday baskets are available, which make great personal and business gifts.

Party Express
City Place Transportation Building
8 Park Plaza, Suite 174
Boston, MA 02116
(617) 338-CAKE (2253)
A party and cake delivery/shipping service. Contact Glynn Kalil.

Wonton Food Inc.
220-222 Moore St.
Brooklyn, NY 11206
(800) 776-8889
Fax: (718) 628-7788
Personalized fortune cookies; 15¢each; 400 minimum.

Wine Design
2112 Auburn Lane
Wilmington, NC 28405-6209
(800) 201-9463
Customized wine and champagne labels.

PART FIVE

PRO BONO: CIVIC MARKETING

FoURteEN

CONTRIBUTE TO COMPLEMENTARY CAUSES

There's nothing wrong with doing well from doing good.
JOHN BRYANT, FOUNDER (AFTER THE LOS ANGELES RIOTS)
OF OPERATION HOPE

1. Help others, help your business.
2. Look for the perfect fit.
3. Ask your customers and employees what's important to them.

What's one of the newest, smartest ways for a small business to market itself? By pooling its resources and strategically donating time and effort to one cause. Nancy Michaels coined a word for it: Civic Marketing.

With more and more people—and businesses—interested in social responsibility, the days of *only* making financial donations are over. Ronnie Dragoon, owner of Ben's Delicatessen in Hicksville, New York, knows all about marketing his business in clever and socially responsible ways. First, Dragoon purchased an old ambulance from a local fire department, then doctored it up to become Ben's Kosher Ambulance. As an extension of the delicatessen, the ambulance is rented for private parties, fundraisers, and barbecues—an unusual way to set Ben's apart and make it more visible. But the *pièce de résistance* is Dragoon's "Pint for a Pint" Civic Marketing campaign that ties into local blood-donation agencies. When someone donates a pint of blood, the attending agency gives each donor a coupon for a free pint of chicken soup from Ben's. Dragoon believes that his Civic Marketing campaign offers his business more exposure, and also helps others.

1. HELP OTHERS, HELP YOUR BUSINESS.

Mary Lou Andre, president of Organization By Design in Needham, Massachusetts, also embodies what Civic Marketing is all about. Andre is a fashion consultant, and a dresser of numerous TV anchors; in addition she donates her time to a local shelter for homeless women. Andre has organized the shelter's donation area, which is filled with cast-off clothing, and has helped homeless women put together outfits that are appropriate for job interviews. "I'm strategic, and wanted to leverage my efforts to benefit a nonprofit organization and my business," says Andre. "I knew that I had a lot to give and made a commitment to give back to a shelter for women."

Andre also enlisted the Girl Scouts to iron and put away clothing for the guests of the shelter. They put goodie bags together with toiletries and makeup to welcome the women. "At one time I packed a suitcase for every graduate of the program to help plan a wardrobe based on their employment needs," she says. Andre also takes unwanted clothing from her clients and donates it to the shelter.

It's a savvy idea, and an unusual one that probably only she, as a fashion consultant, would have thought of—thus creating a special niche for her business. In fact, her civic-mindedness has set Andre apart from her competition. "It's difficult to qualify, but my volunteer work separates me from the pack," Andre says.

CIVIC MARKETING REWARDS ARE ONGOING.

What are the rewards of Andre's civic-mindedness? "Publicity, an expanded client base, increased credibility, and a softened image," says Andre. "It has me perceived as a caring and contributing member of the community. It is also a stress-reducer to offer my service in a nontraditional way."

Andre is right; although Civic Marketing is sometimes overlooked, it's a smart way for your business to be known, seen, and trusted in your community. But it's different from the other marketing strategies outlined in this book, which are implemented to directly improve the bottom line. Civic Marketing is in a class all by itself; its altruistic purpose is to help others while you ultimately help yourself and your business. Your efforts benefit others, with the hope that they may also inspire employee and customer loyalty, and eventually pave the way for increased profits.

HELP OTHERS WHILE HELPING YOURSELF.

CIVIC MARKETING "GIVES BACK" AND ALSO:

- Fosters goodwill
- Creates a positive impression and puts you, the business owner, in the role of a leader
- May inspire customer loyalty and improve employee morale
- Distinguishes your business from the competition, as you become known, seen, recognized, trusted, and remembered
- Establishes your credibility
- Creates win-win situations

Although it can, Civic Marketing doesn't necessarily involve donations of money, which is why it's perfect for small businesses.

"If you support your community, it will support you," says Jill Smith, who founded Buckeye Beans & Herbs in Spokane, Washington, with husband, Doug. The Smiths, who were named that state's Small Business Persons of the Year in 1996, began Civic Marketing with Habitat for Humanity. Their successful concept was to sell tree- and heart-shaped pastas and donate a portion of the profits to the charitable organization. "I walked my walk," says Jill. "Because of our involvement with Habitat for Humanity, we gained more recognition in the city, although that's not why we did it.... Newspaper editors loved this stuff, as it gave us a profile in the community.... It gave us recognition, praise, emotional payback, and the community saw Buckeye Beans as a desirable place to work."

Fagier Blackwell of Burlington, North Carolina, concurs. Blackwell, who was the first black owner of a floral shop in his county, now owns several thriving businesses. He is a member of an AIDS advocacy group and past president of the downtown co-op. Recently he accepted an invitation to be the grand marshall of an AIDS awareness parade. "I don't think I lost any business," Blackwell says. "Any business that I've lost I've probably doubled from people who say, 'Hey, I like what he stands for.'"

WHY DO BUSINESSES ENGAGE IN CIVIC MARKETING?

A national survey reveals why. The survey, which asked opinions of executives from seventy companies, was released in April of 1996; it was commissioned by Cone Communications, Boston, and conducted by Roper Search Worldwide.

- 93 percent want to build better relationships with customers
- 89 percent feel it enhances corporate image and reputation
- 61 percent want to create a new platform
- 59 percent want to maintain or create a compelling corporate purpose

Only half of those surveyed say increasing sales is a major reason to do cause-related marketing.

"The findings from this survey show that increasing sales is not the primary motivation of executives who have successfully implemented cause-related marketing programs at their companies," said Cone CEO Carol Cone in a press release. "Building long-lasting bonds with customers and developing a unique corporate image in a competitive marketplace are much more important reasons."

In another study, by Frankel & Company, 69 percent of consumers say they've taken part in a marketing promotion because of its cause tie-in.

If cause-related marketing, as exemplified by IBM and its sponsorship of the Olympics, was the buzzword for the Eighties, Civic Marketing defines the Nineties and the future beyond. It is another secret for self-made success. It *can* involve financial donations, but more frequently deals with contributions of time, energy, and effort.

GIVE AND GET.

"My motto is To give is to gain," says Ray Bastarache, president of Barter Network in Milford, Connecticut, which he founded, in 1985, at age twenty-four. Bastarache, the 1989 State of Connecticut Entrepreneur of the Year, realized that bartering could be an effective way to help charities. The company sought donations in trade, which were given to the local chapter of the Boy Scouts. "This way we generate extra revenue for the Boy Scouts, which they can spend on various goods and services, anything from accommodations to printing services," he says. Bastarache also initiated a successful program whereby companies bartered products and services in exchange for tuition vouchers to send needy students to a Connecticut technical school.

Bastarache realizes that Civic Marketing offers advantages to charities—and to his business. "We get publicity from it, but that's not the motivation," Bastarache says. "It generates a positive public image. Bartering doesn't have the best image in the industry. It's young—our industry is probably twenty years old—and it has attracted companies that have gone out of business." But Civic Marketing, according to Bastarache, allows his business to put its best foot forward.

Think that you don't need to bother with civic causes? Then listen to Barry Potekin, founder of Chicago's wildly successful Gold Coast Dogs restaurant chain, and *Venture* magazine's 1987 Entrepreneur of the Year. A brief history: at age forty, after bad investments lost all of his money, and that of his parents, the former stockbroker staged a comeback with a new concept: an upscale fast-food restaurant. Today, he's a changed man. "The first time around I took and took," says Potekin. "I was arrogant and obnoxious. Now I do favors for people."

Nowadays, Potekin donates $10,000 annually to Chicago homeless shelters, and about $15,000 each year to the Make-A-Wish Foundation. Since, in the process, he became a motivational speaker, Potekin also visits hospitals to talk to young addicts and offer words of hope. In addition he gives gratis speeches to the MBA programs at the University of Illinois and DePaul University. "The better you do, the more you have to give back," Potekin says. "It makes me feel better. After all, what goes around, comes around."

In Boise, Idaho, David Lakhani owns a business consulting firm, the Small Business Network. He created a worthy Civic-Marketing project for one of his clients, an art gallery called Decorcreations. Lakhani persuaded Decorcreations to host a wine-tasting during the area's weekly "gallery stroll" and to donate 5 percent of everything sold that evening toward Boise's Family Advocacy Program to assist abused women and children. "It's a great way to get people into the gallery," says Lakhani. "But more important, people who support the Family Advocacy program support people who support them."

Interested? Here's how to start a Civic Marketing project of your own.

Aligning your business with complementary causes helps to imprint your product or service in the minds of customers. Sy Sperling knows all about it. You know, Sy Sperling—he's not only the Hair Club for Men president, he's also a client? For the past ten years, Sperling has quietly donated hundreds of free hair weaves to children undergoing chemotherapy or radiation treatments. It's a perfect fit.

2. LOOK FOR THE PERFECT FIT.

Gary Goldberg, the owner of Gary Goldberg Inc., a successful financial planning company in upstate New York, has also found a complementary fit. He makes cash donations to children's charities for one simple reason: because he is grateful to have three healthy children of his own. Goldberg also donates to the Make-A-Wish Foundation, and annually holds a celebrity golf tournament that gives its profits to a different children's cause. As a result, "the general image of our firm is absolutely enhanced," says Goldberg, a 1988 recipient of a Horatio Alger award. "You want your name associated with positive things."

Causes involved with one's appearance made perfect sense for David Nicholas, one of the top makeup artists in Boston. For five years, Nicholas volunteered his time, services, and products to the city's Shriners Burns Institute, and eventually became a staff member. There, he teaches patients how to improve their appearance and conceal burns and scars with makeup; in fact, 40 percent of his business is volunteer. Today, Nicholas has expanded his good deeds to include three cancer organizations, the Scleroderma Association, the AIDS Action Committee (where he works with patients with Kaposi's sarcoma), as well as organizations devoted to alopecia (hair loss). He's even taught blind people how to apply makeup, using a "touch-and-feel" method." Why does he do it? Nicholas, who openly acknowledges that he is gay, knows all too well the agony of not fitting in. "As a kid, I had bad acne.... I wasn't accepted and I had no friends. Looking back on the pain of rejection and neglect," he says, "I figured that these people must go through even worse.... I see such pain." Nicholas found that his Civic Marketing eventually improved his bottom line, even though he says, "that's not why I do it." However, his

Points to remember:

- Work with causes you believe in.
- Offer something different.
- Donate within your industry.

donation of services had a positive effect: "It caused me to become known quicker within my industry than if I had done things in the 'normal' way," he says.

WHAT WORKS FOR YOUR BUSINESS?

If your business:

- Caters to families (bookstore, day care)...consider supporting youth sports, child welfare projects, literacy.
- Involves food (restaurant, caterer, coffee shop, grocer)...consider supporting food banks, shelters, soup kitchens.
- Appeals to women (beauty parlor, aerobics)...consider supporting spousal abuse programs, shelters.
- Targets animals (pet store, groomer)...consider supporting endangered species, animal shelters, rescue leagues.
- Involves the outdoors (gardening shop, nursery)...consider supporting

- rainforest, global warming, adopt-a-highway, recycling programs.
- Repairs computers...consider donating used computers to schools or other charities.
- Is an accounting firm...consider donating time to help senior citizens prepare taxes.
- Is a clothing store...consider supporting Goodwill, the Salvation Army, and other charities that clothe the needy.
- Is a graphic-design firm...consider supporting arts programs, cultural activities for children, and inner-city kids.
- Is a health-food store or fitness club...consider supporting disease research or fitness associations.

Dave Thomas, founder of Wendy's, found a cause that really hit home. Thomas, adopted as a child, is a national adoption advocate who travels extensively generating awareness for the cause. "How did I get involved with adoption?" Thomas asks. "I was adopted, so I understand how important it is to have a home and family....I'm very active in promoting adoption and Wendy's International, and many of our franchisees support local adoption programs, too. To support employees who choose to adopt, Wendy's employee benefit program provides up to five thousand dollars to help defray adoption fees."

Personal reasons aside, Thomas also cites another reason for his Civic Marketing program: "You have a responsibility to give back, to support the community that supports your business," he says. "Besides, it's the right thing to do."

In Holland, Michigan, G. W. Haworth has used a similar strategy. His company, Haworth Inc., is the world's second-largest manufacturer of office furniture and seating, and in 1993 was named one of the one hundred best companies to work for. When Haworth founded his company, he had no money to donate, so he only volunteered his time to worthy causes. However, his firm recently donated furnishings for a conference center, administrative offices, and dormitories at Michigan's Hope College, as well as $4 million to build the Haworth Conference and Learning Center there. His goal is "to open up the city to meeting rooms and bring in the civic leaders and unite the business and college community," Haworth says.

Common sense, in most cases, will reveal the best organizations that your business can donate its time or profits to. In Sperling's case, for example, the donation of hair weaves to chemotherapy patients makes perfect sense. What if your company is the world's Number One maker of widgets? Here's how to go about deciding on an appropriate Civic Marketing pursuit.

COMPILE A GENERAL LIST OF ORGANIZATIONS THAT MIGHT BE RIGHT FOR YOUR BUSINESS

First, make a list of your business goals. Then brainstorm and try to find organizations that have the same goals or the same "cause." (See p. 164 for resources.) A widget company—or for our purposes, let's say a manufacturer of nails—should think about aligning with companies involved in construction. List the for-profit construction companies, and the causes that *they* donate to. Or simply find nonprofit construction companies. In this case, for example, a good fit might be Habitat for Humanity, a philanthropic organization founded by former President Jimmy Carter that builds homes for the needy.

INCLUDE NONPROFIT ORGANIZATIONS IN YOUR COMMUNITY

Yet another strategy is to review the nonprofit and community-based organizations that you, or your company, feel a strong connection to, or which may need your help, as did Andre.

SEEK A NATURAL MATCH BASED ON YOUR PERSONAL EXPERIENCE OR THAT OF YOUR EMPLOYEES

Sperling's donation of hair weaves is an excellent example of a "natural" match based on his personal experience, as is the Dave Thomas example.

ATTEND MEETINGS OF NEIGHBORHOOD ASSOCIATIONS TO DISCOVER LOCAL CONCERNS

If you attend meetings of neighborhood associations, you can learn about the people who live and work in your community, and their concerns. This way, you will take the pulse of your community and discover the challenging issues being faced. For example, if your community is considering a curfew to keep kids off the street at night, your business might contribute funds to build a youth center or outfit a Girls or Boys Club. Whatever you do, make sure to commit for more than a year to have the most impact. (More on this later.)

STICK TO SOMETHING YOU'RE FAMILIAR WITH.

3. ASK YOUR CUSTOMERS AND EMPLOYEES WHAT'S IMPORTANT TO THEM.

Since one of the goals of Civic Marketing is to foster goodwill in the minds of your customers, it makes sense to go to them first and to ask them about the causes they're most interested in. It's also a smart tactic to conduct a sample survey, asking customers about the organizations and causes that are important to them. Include these questions:

Which would you like us to support?

____Community programs

____Statewide programs

____National programs

____International programs

Where would you like our resources to go?

____Youth

____Environment

____Animals

____Health

____Disease prevention/cures

____Schools

____Violence prevention

____Public safety

____Racial and ethnic understanding

____Poverty

____Other_____

What do you perceive as being the dominant issues in the community? (e.g., youth violence, drop-out rates, pollution, public safety)_____

Would you rather see us:

____Donate profits

____Volunteer time

____Donate equipment

____Provide gratis service

TELL YOUR CUSTOMERS

Use advertising and in-store signs to tell the community about your Civic Marketing. The simple words, "We're proud supporters of," together with the name of the charity, is all it takes.

THE ADVANTAGES OF EMPLOYEE PARTICIPATION IN YOUR CIVIC MARKETING

No doubt about it, Civic Marketing can also improve employee morale, if you make the necessary efforts to involve your employees. How do you inspire your employees to participate in your Civic Marketing program?

First, *acknowledge and reward employee efforts* in a visible and public manner. In doing so, you support their contributions, and also recognize them as valuable members of your company. For example, you might sponsor a contest for the most significant employee contributions, then honor all your employees with a summer outing at a team-building camp, or simply hold an "Employee of the Month" pizza party for everyone involved. The actual "winners" would receive tangible rewards such as a half-day off at their discretion, dinner-for-two at a favorite restaurant, a store gift certificate, or the funding to attend a business workshop or seminar.

Second, if your business can afford it, *make a cash contribution to the community organization of your employee's choice.* You might even donate a portion of gross sales to it, during your employee's "recognition month." When your employees are satisfied, you boost morale, increase productivity, and decrease turnover—which all positively affect your bottom line. What could be better than that?

Third, *allow your employees to donate their time on your time.* For example, they might donate their services to a soup kitchen during lunchtime and an hour thereafter—while still on the clock with your business.

Jim Berluti would be the first to tell you that it's important for his employees to see him "walk the walk." Berluti is president and CEO of Eastern Connection, a business-to-business express parcel service based in Wellesley, Massachusetts. Each year the company participates in the American Heart Association's "Hearts in Bloom" floral bouquet fundraiser, "which used to be a tremendous cost and a logistical nightmare for them," Berluti says. Berluti volunteered Eastern Connection's delivery services, and his own. "I'm out there with the foot couriers, even during snowstorms," Berluti says. "It builds camaraderie." Furthermore, after donating money to the Special Olympics held in 1995 in Connecticut, Berluti discovered that some of his employees had similarly donated their time. "One of our employees was even a caddy," he says proudly.

Steve Belkin, founder of Trans National Group, Boston, puts his money where his mouth is. He devotes 50 percent of his time to charities including the United Way, Harvard Business School, Sports Museum of New England, Combined Jewish Philanthropies and Anti-Defamation League. He has also instituted a special Charities Committee at his business, whereby employees nominate up to forty charitable causes for consideration; from there everyone in the company votes on five and nominates a sponsor. Those five committee members then bring in a member of the charity for a meeting and planning session. Belkin has found that, as a result of his program, "more than fifty percent of our employees donate their time and make a personal contribution."

How to get your employees involved? If your company consists of fewer than four employees, you should take an informal poll about the civic causes they are most interested in contributing to. Larger firms can set up a suggestion box where employees can submit proposals. Your firm might also take requests from current clients. By encouraging the opinions and suggestions from employees and customers, you are, in fact, encouraging their own civic entrepreneurship.

MAKE A DIFFERENCE

Inspired employees can also be found in Jupiter, Florida, where the staff of RJ Gator's restaurant follows the example of their company founder, Tim Timoteo. "Our mission statement," says Timoteo, "is to be the best neighborhood restaurant in the United States, and to make a difference in every community we're in." Timoteo does numerous things to inspire his staff; among other things, he dresses up as Santa Claus at Christmas and delivers toys to community centers. Plus, "every opening of RJ Gator's benefits a local charity, Little League ball team, or high school band," he adds. On Thanksgiving, Timoteo closes all of his restaurants in order to feed the needy. "My staff and customers all volunteer their time. It gets them involved," Timoteo says. "They get so much out of it; they all want to work on Thanksgiving Day." When the company sponsors bowling contests to benefit Junior Achievement, the team that raises the most money also gets a prize such as dinner-for-two or a gift certificate for sporting goods.

Have your own special Civic Marketing plan? The next chapter shows you how to get it started.

Points to remember:

- Make a difference.
- Follow the traditional road, too.
- Offer incentives to civic-minded employees.

Fifteen

DEVELOP YOUR OWN UNIQUE CIVIC MARKETING PLAN

If you haven't got charity in your heart, you have the worst kind of heart problem.
BOB HOPE

1. Charity begins at home.
2. Be the solution, not the problem.
3. Commit for at least one year, and maximize your exposure.

If you can't discover an ideal fit—and in some cases, even if you can—it sometimes makes sense to start your own campaign. Besides, the more unique your efforts, the more likely that the idea can't be copied.

Tom Ivory, owner of the Philadelphia-based Baker Street Stores, knows all about it. Ivory and his brother Tim created a company that would combine sound business principles with socially responsible philosophies.

Rather than using conventional marketing, Baker Street sponsors Civic Marketing programs such as Butts for Baguettes, which is timed in conjunction with the American Cancer Society's Great American Smokeout. The Ivorys saw it as the perfect opportunity to advertise their bakery and simultaneously make a statement about the dangers of smoking. It encourages customers to bring in a pack of cigarettes (open or unopened) to the bakery, throw them into the garbage, and receive a complimentary baguette for kicking their habit. To advertise the event, Baker Street uses store signage to announce the promotion, alongside advertising provided by the American Cancer Society.

As a result, Baker Street has received free media coverage from one of the local television affiliates. Tom estimates that the free advertising could well have cost more than $20,000.

The Ivorys also help promote local civic organizations by allowing one at a time to have "free run" of the bakery for a day. The civic group decides what to sell and promote; the Ivorys provide staff and facility, and also divide their bakery profits. They describe the idea as "raising dough for a neighbor's day." They believe that their Civic Marketing generates traffic at the bakery, and also promotes goodwill and community awareness.

1. CHARITY BEGINS AT HOME.

Nadine Heaps, an independent insurance sales agent in Ashland, Massachusetts, also found a special way to inspire loyalty in her customers and in her community. If anything, Heaps is something of a local philanthropist.

Heaps launched Ashland Partners in Education (APIE) with Ashland High School, area businesses, senior citizens, and members of the community; its goal was to network and improve the quality of education and services at the high school. The 125 attendees at each of the three breakfast meetings lobbied to receive such donations as thirty laptop computers and two drafting machines. Heaps also hired three high school students to work for her part-time. "It's just a win-win situation for everyone," Heaps says. "I enjoy teaching these students about what will be expected of them in a professional situation and they enjoy the responsibility and salary that goes along with being a valued employee."

Heaps also combined APIE with another program that she introduced, "Attitude of Gratitude," in which she donates a percentage of her gross monthly proceeds to a community-based organization. The causes vary depending on identified needs; her recent contributions include sending a group of fourth-grade students on a field trip to Washington, D.C., and donating funds to purchase a talking computer for a speech-impaired ten-year-old student in her community. "It's neat that people in my community know that I've made a commitment to my town," says Heaps.

Michelle Araujo, a twenty-three-year-old woman with three children, completed the "mini-MBA" program offered by the nonprofit National Foundation for Teaching Entrepreneurship. Today, Araujo is a shining example of NFTE's success—and an inspiration. Araujo founded A La Mode Fashions in New Bedford, Massachusetts, and now has embarked on a Civic Marketing program of her own. Araujo donates 10 percent of her proceeds to on-campus organizations that sponsor flea markets where she sells her clothes. "My story is deviant," says Araujo. "If I was a rich girl this story wouldn't be as compelling. I don't fit the profile of a successful, young business owner. I'm a single mother with three children still on welfare who grew up in the projects and is working every day to create a productive life."

2. BE THE SOLUTION, NOT THE PROBLEM.

When it comes to giving back, no one does it better than Steve Mariotti. In 1981 five teenagers mugged him for ten dollars; rather than retaliate, Mariotti turned the experience into a victory. The financial whiz and former international financial analyst at Ford Motor Company gave up his own import-export business to teach in the rough neighborhoods his muggers called home. His first job was at Boys & Girls High School in the Bedford-Stuyvesant area of Brooklyn. There, Mariotti discovered that the only way to interest his disadvantaged students was to teach them about owning their own businesses—thus empowering them. Mariotti demystified business concepts and offered hands-on experience. He taught the how-tos of buying low at wholesale and selling high, record-keeping, marketing, even how to read the *Wall Street Journal*. He soon discovered that his students' challenging lives, filled with uncertainty and risk, had the same qualities that characterized entrepreneurs. By 1988, when assigned to a school in Fort Apache, "everything went right," Mariotti says. Backed by his entrepreneurial techniques, "every kid had a business," be it babysitting, caring for the elderly, repairing bikes, painting, or selling Avon products. "They started acting like Harvard Business School types," says Mariotti. "Their humanity came out. It was the most beautiful thing I ever saw in my life."

Mariotti's efforts were so successful that he founded the National Foundation for Teaching Entrepreneurship, Inc. (NFTE, pronounced "nifty"). This national nonprofit organization teaches inner-city youths, including the physically challenged and those in detention, about business. Through special training programs, NFTE has taught more than twenty-nine thousand students the fundamentals of entrepreneurship in Boston, Chicago, New York, and as far away as Glasgow, Scotland. "Business can be used to help people who are in pain because they can't make money," Mariotti adds.

OTHER WAYS TO DONATE

- Participate in a telethon.
- Purchase tickets to fundraisers.
- Donate your product or service to a silent auction.
- Hold special events.
- Have a holiday open house.
- Celebrate your anniversary date of doing business. Charge a minimal admission and donate a portion of the proceeds to a specific charity.
- Collect clothing for the needy.
- Organize a food drive.
- Visit local pediatric wards, nursing homes, and schools.
- Join forces with other area businesses to make a contribution.
- Support community fundraisers. For example, if the local high school band is seeking financial support, you can hold a "high school band night" whereby a portion of your profits from one or two days are donated to them. Or donate a special gift that can be raffled off, with the proceeds going to the fundraiser.

3. COMMIT FOR AT LEAST ONE YEAR, AND MAXIMIZE YOUR EXPOSURE.

It's important to make a commitment for at least one year; hit-and-run contributions may provide a quick fix, but the most reward for you and your cause will occur over time, through repeated efforts.

John Sayles and Sheree Clark, owners of Sayles Graphic Design firm in Des Moines, Iowa, advise: "Think of it as a long-term approach." They use Civic Marketing for "fame, fortune, or fun—we'll take two out of three," say the two principals. "We have several pro-bono and nonprofit clients. We give our talent and our time as well." They have donated to the local zoo, the Des Moines Art Center, Planned Parenthood, and the Boys and Girls Club, among other organizations. "The main reason we contribute to civic-related causes," says Clark, "is that it's good business. It helps us to retain good client relationships and people know who gives and who doesn't. It needs to be a cause we believe in or have a connection to, or that our clients are affiliated with. For instance, if a client is on the board of directors of an art museum, and asks us to help the museum, we'll do it. We also advise small design firms and freelancers that volunteering your services can eventually lead to paying jobs down the road."

Next, after you have created an ongoing presence with your philanthropy through donations of time, energy, or even money, make sure to let the public know.

Sy Sperling can tell you why. Although Sperling donated Hair Club for Men services for ten years to cancer-ravaged children without any publicity, he recently decided to use radio to spread the word. "My original motivation was strictly altruistic," says Sperling. "But now, after ten years, why not take credit for it? Most religions say that if the end is good, why not take a pat on the back? I think we deserve the credit. It brings a dollar into our bank account so we can give ten cents back. If you're not successful, you can't help others."

Richard Field would concur; the owner of a gourmet food and wine store in Hawaii, Field has worked tirelessly on the annual "Taste of Honolulu" that promotes wine and also raises money for Easter Seals. "Only in the last four or five years did we start to promote our participation," says Field. "What happened is that the perception of the store has changed," he says. "We no longer have the image of being 'just another liquor store.' More and more people point to us and say, 'They're the guys putting on the event.'"

Informing existing and prospective customers about your endeavors helps to showcase your business in a good light and create a positive image—an added bonus. Let's face it—nowadays, people want to patronize businesses that are socially responsible. Besides, your contributions also publicize the charity, and that's yet another advantage.

How else can you get the word out? Try some of these ideas.

ISSUE A PROCLAMATION

Randy Barth, a DJ who founded Rack-A-Disc (now known as Premier Talent Group), did just that with his "Just Say No Locomotion Promotion." The Massachusetts high school drug-awareness program was more than your average dance; using closed-circuit cameras and a ten-foot video screen, the "locomotion promotion" gave teens an opportunity to tell their friends why they don't do drugs. "It was so powerful," says Barth. "Kids went to the mike, telling their friends how they lost friends and relatives to drugs." The dance also included a lip synch contest and a thirty-second commercial that showed kids chanting "I'm drug-free." To promote the event, Barth worked with the National Recreation and Parks Association, which, in turn, got the *coup de grâce*: then-Governor Michael Dukakis issued a proclamation declaring September 29, 1990, as "Locomotion Promotion Day." The event generated "tons of publicity," says Barth. "It gave us more clout."

USE YOUR OWN NEWSLETTER

Remember Mary Lou Andre? She lets the world know about her charitable efforts through her newsletter. "I send my newsletter to every member of each organization I belong to," Andre states. "I consider the exposure an opportunity because if you really are a giver, you get. I've been featured in publicity with nonprofit organizations to which I've donated my time. I love to give back, but there's an element of excitement to leveraging my efforts."

MENTION YOUR CONTRIBUTIONS IN YOUR ADVERTISING

If you advertise in your local newspaper, why not mention your support of the Little League team or donation to the soup kitchen? It may prompt a reader to seek out your business over that of your competition.

SEND PRESS RELEASES AND PHOTOS TO THE MEDIA

Describe your company's Civic Marketing activities—perhaps your employees have cleaned up the neighborhood, or maybe you've presided at a ribbon-cutting ceremony for a playground you've funded. Write a press release and invite the media to the ribbon-cutting event, or just send a press release with a photo. Who knows? You may find yourself the subject of a feature story.

Adds Steve Mariotti, founder of the National Foundation for Teaching Entrepreneurship (NFTE): "I try to teach reporters the difficulties of the field, and educate them on the whole industry.... I don't just give an interview; I try to make them an expert in the field.... I write thank-you letters, I stay in touch with them. I return phone calls immediately. And I try not to ever exaggerate."

SPONSOR AN AWARD

It not only fosters goodwill but may generate publicity and be the topic of numerous conversations! Haley Garrison of Williamsburg, Virginia, has implemented this successful Civic Marketing strategy for the past seven years. The owner of a company that deals in collectible antique stocks and bonds, Garrison annually bestows a prize to the top business student at his alma mater, the Virginia Military Academy, who has the characteristics of becoming a future Captain of Industry. The award is a magnificently framed antique security with a plaque bearing the name of the award and the honored recipient. In Garrison's eyes, this is a win-win situation, as it spreads the word about his unusual company, and also honors a top student with a reward for his hard work.

GET YOUR PROJECT WRITTEN ABOUT IN NEWSLETTERS OTHER THAN YOUR OWN

If you're contributing to the Special Olympics, chances are they communicate through a variety of publications, such as a newsletter. This is a great opportunity to let their readership know about your contribution.

OFFER TO PRODUCE A COMMUNITY-ACCESS TV SHOW OR APPEAR ON A PROGRAM

Go on-air with a member of a community organization, which your business is supporting, to talk about the difference your business contributions of time and/or money have made. If you can enlist other organizations to join your efforts, and also appear on the program, you will position yourself as an effective business leader. Kim Whittaker, for instance, appeared as a guest on one of Boston Neighborhood Network's cable programs to explain her concept of Baby Faire—a consumer expo geared to prospective parents that is now in four markets—and her donations to a civic cause. Whittaker donates 10 percent of her proceeds to Success by Six, a community-wide effort whose goal is to prepare children to enter school healthy and ready to succeed by age six. The advantage of such an appearance is that it further exposed Baby Faire and Whittaker's civic contributions to a larger audience that may not have known about it.

USE YOUR COMPANY FOYER, LOBBY, OR WINDOWS AS A SHOWCASE FOR YOUR EFFORTS

If your business has received any awards for its civic activities, make sure to display them. Likewise, if your firm's civic projects have been profiled in a newsletter, newspaper, or magazine, reprint them and frame them for prominent display so your new and prospective customers will get the message.

With strategic use of Civic Marketing, you're automatically positioning your company as a do-gooder with a purpose. Since your efforts are not completely self-serving, and you have a natural tie-in to the organization that you are donating your time and resources to, you automatically set the stage to attract media attention. Now you need to learn how to pitch story ideas, respond to media requests, and develop lifelong relationships. That's what the next five chapters are all about.

PART FIVE RESOURCES:

Visit your local library to research professional and not-for-profit associations in these directories:

Encyclopedia of Associations
Gale Research
Book Tower
Detroit, MI 48226

National Trade and Professional Associations of the United States
1350 New York Ave., NW
Washington, D.C. 20005

PRESS WALTZ: HOW TO ATTRACT THE MEDIA

SixteEN

PAY FOR ADVERTISING; PRAY FOR PUBLICITY

I knew nothing about marketing. I just wanted the inn to get noticed. I discovered that was called marketing.
DEEDY MARBLE, FORMER OWNER OF THE GOVERNOR'S INN, LUDLOW, VERMONT, THE 1987 "INN OF THE YEAR"

1. Create credibility.
2. Show your talents; know the times.
3. Set the stage for media attention.

There's an old adage that says that you *pay* for advertising but *pray* for publicity. Nothing could be more true. Both advertising and media publicity offer visibility, but they are very different.

Paid advertising is a time-honored way to let customers know what you offer, but positive press coverage does something no ad can: it gives people faith in you. Let's face it, Americans are a pretty skeptical bunch when it comes to advertising claims. We're much more likely to believe information from a news story.

Besides, readers tend to pay closer attention to news stories whereas they give ads just three to nine seconds of their time, according to an old advertising maxim. News stories demand more of our attention and have greater credibility because of the perception that they have been "screened" by editors.

1. CREATE CREDIBILITY.

Credibility is the buzzword that gets the public to put their trust in you. Think about your own experiences: What do you put more faith in—an ad, or an article you read in a magazine? The answer is obvious: the story.

A print or broadcast story not only offers much more exposure than an ad; it costs only time, not money. Plus, press attention begets press attention. When you are quoted or featured in one story, chances are you will be quoted or featured in other stories. According to the Public Relations Society of America, approximately 80 percent of news stories are generated by outside sources—meaning, people like you and me. So if you manufacture a great product, offer an innovative service, or have a compelling story to tell, by all means let the press know about it. They always have space and airtime to fill—and with luck, they will choose information about you and your business.

However, there is one obvious disadvantage of free publicity over paid advertising: you have no control over what is written about you. What most businesses fear is bad press coverage. As another PR sage once remarked, "there's no such thing as bad publicity." It's hard to believe, but even bad publicity can be good; you just have to look at the increased sales of Ford Broncos—by 14 percent—after O. J. Simpson's famous car chase, to realize that it's true.[1] The only thing worse than being badly written about is not being written about at all!

Points to remember:

- Advertising and media publicity offer visibility—but only publicity offers credibility.
- Pursuing media exposure costs you time, not cash.
- Press attention usually snowballs, leading to even more coverage.

[1] *Parade* magazine, Dec. 31, 1995, p. 6.

IF THEY CAN'T SAY SOMETHING NICE...

ADVERTISING VS. PUBLICITY

Advertising	Publicity
Immediate results if consistently placed	Immediate and long-term results
You control content	You have no control
You are the sole focus of the ad	You may have to share the spotlight with a competitor or those with opposing views
You can target your audience	Broad audience, who may not be potential customers
Not inherently believable	Gives you credibility
Inadequate medium to explain complex ideas and concepts	Allows you to convey complex ideas and concepts
Limited lifespan	Leaves an enduring impression
Costly	Cost-effective

Here's how to learn the ropes, work within the system, and reap the returns! If you follow in the footsteps of some successful entrepreneurs, you and the press can cha-cha and make beautiful music together.

2. KNOW YOUR TALENTS; KNOW THE TIMES.

In the early 1990s the United States suffered from a serious recession, and the Northeast was hit particularly hard. However, this distressing fact of life didn't have too much impact on Jim and Amy Dacyczyn (pronounced "decision") of Leeds, Maine; the couple are self-described tightwads who, on a $30,000 salary, have been able to afford six children, an eleven-room farmhouse, and savings for college tuition. After years of contemplating potential businesses, Amy brainstormed one day and the idea of a newsletter on tightwaddery popped into her head. "It just clicked—it just seemed to work," Amy says. She went with her gut—and did something different.

Amy's timing couldn't have been more perfect. Americans, at that time, were dealing with the recession and looking for ways to cut back and spend less. *The Tightwad Gazette* was the answer to many people's problems.

After coming up with the big idea, the Dacyczyns went to work. They made some mistakes along the way, such as placing ads for *The Tightwad Gazette* in *Yankee* magazine and *Mother Earth News*, which barely broke even. Free copies distributed at doctor's offices also proved inefficient, as did an incentive plan whereby current subscribers got a free month of the newsletter when they referred another subscriber.

FOR TIGHTWADS, THEY SURE SPENT A LOT.

Then came the Big Idea: a friend suggested to Amy that she send a press release to the media. A press release? "I never would have considered it because I wasn't a professional writer," says Amy. "I never thought that the legitimate literary community would look at me as being credible."

However, at her friend's insistence, Amy sent about fourteen releases to newspapers in Maine, whose names she compiled at the library from *Gale's Directory of Media*. "Actually, it was more of a letter than a press release," Amy says. "We felt that the newsletter spoke for itself, so we wrote an amusing letter and sent it out with three past issues of the newsletter." The result? Two responses from the mailing and two articles about the newsletter in Maine newspapers. These small publications are usually the bricks that build larger stories in bigger publications.

PITCH YOUR IDEAS TO THE PRESS.

One article, which was published in the *Maine Sunday Telegram*, was written by reporter Brad Lemley, who felt certain that he could sell the story to *Parade* magazine. He did; it ran on March 17, 1991, and the rest is history. In just one week of their intense media blitz, Amy and Jim appeared on *Donahue*, *CBS This Morning*, *Today*, and *The Home Show*.

Says Amy: "On our peak media days we received the largest response of about twenty-five thousand from the *Parade* story alone....We received national exposure because we had a unique business tailored to the changing economic times, which was relevant to people's concerns about the environment."

The peak of their subscription base reached 104,000 subscribers, who each paid twelve dollars a year for a subscription. Their first book, *The Tightwad Gazette I,* was on the *New York Times* bestseller list for four weeks and sold 300,000 copies.

Since that time *The Tightwad Gazette* has evolved into three books (which all sold a total of 500,000 copies) and millions of dollars for the Dacyczyns—who still abide by their tightwad ways. (In December 1996, they ceased publication of the newsletter in order to pursue other interests.)

The Dacyczyns are the perfect example of how ordinary people, with absolutely no publicity budget, can receive media coverage that mushrooms into national exposure and millions of dollars. Their experience shows that other small businesses can achieve similar results. If they could do it, so can you!

But before we explain exactly how *you* can be a media magnet, let us offer a brief overview of how the media works.

A FEW WORDS OF WISDOM

Yes, you may have a good thing—an excellent product or service. But if no one knows about it....What's the point? Media coverage is one of the most powerful marketing tools available. Not only does it spread the word about your company, it also enhances your credibility, improves your image, and has the potential to boost your business.

Positive press coverage may not guarantee fame and fortune, but it can offer swift passage from obscurity to prominence. No other medium carries the weight of the independent press.

Therefore, a story about you or your company will influence people as nothing else can.

3. SET THE STAGE FOR MEDIA ATTENTION.

OK…. So your company makes the world's best, new titanium widgets. It begs the million-dollar question: How do you get your business mentioned in the media? How do you turn it into a story that attracts media coverage? Well, in our media-saturated culture, there's not a whole lot that *hasn't* been brought to our attention. The trick lies in the *presentation*. Spin your story in an original way and it will feel fresh. Think in terms of "sound bites." Form your story idea to appeal to as broad an audience as possible. And make sure that it fits into one of the time-tested "hooks" that usually make editors and producers bite: stories that fall under categories that include Trend, Anti-trend, Human Interest, Offbeat, and Public Service, to name a few.

The efforts of Deedy Marble, former innkeeper of The Governor's Inn in Ludlow, Vermont, provide a case study, in a nutshell, of how to successfully publicize a small business, using all the angles and marketing tools. (Deedy sold the inn in February 1999.)

When she and her husband Charlie bought the inn in 1982, they had never even *stayed* in an inn. Yet Deedy instinctively knew what needed to be done to reap visitors. "My friends say I have this innate ability to say, 'Look at me, look at me,'" Deedy says with a laugh.

GET THEIR ATTENTION.

The first thing she did was to write to Kakas, a Boston furrier whose print ads always featured models at a historic location. "They called back the next day," says Deedy, and The Governor's Inn was photographed in September, which brought a flood of good business to the inn.

KEEP YOUR EYES AND EARS OPEN.

In 1982, "I started a press kit, which was unknown for an inn," says Deedy. After qualifying for a bank loan, Deedy also self-published six thousand cookbooks for sixty-three cents a copy, and sold each for five dollars. "Those books went on forever." They brought in exposure that eventually led to a TV segment on *Evening Magazine*, which eventually was rerun nationally.

GET PUBLISHED, GET POPULAR.

After that, "we needed another hook," says Deedy, "so we started a picnic basket." The "Ample Hamper" included filet mignon pâté sandwiches, wine, cheese, and other assorted homemade goodies. Deedy had the hamper professionally photographed, and sent the photos and press releases to the *Boston Globe* and *Yankee*. The next thing she knew the *New York Times* and *Gourmet* both featured it. "That put us over the top," Deedy says. "It was a marketing miracle."

DEVELOP A PRODUCT AND TELL THE PRESS.

By 1987 the inn was voted "Inn of the Year." By 1990 Deedy was invited to speak in Australia at a national conference on tourism—which also brought in business. In 1991, she started a cooking school based on her studies in France and Italy, which has brought guests from as far away as Japan. "We knew we would have to do something remarkable to be noticed," says Deedy.

Points to remember:

- Always look out for opportunities—or create them.
- Create a press kit.
- Develop tie-in products.

In 1997 the inn was named an "Editor's Pick" by *Yankee*'s 1997 Travel Guide to New England. Since its start, the inn has been awarded four stars by the Mobil Travel Guide and has three times been voted one of the nation's ten Best Inns by travel and guidebook writers. Even its phone number is a selling point: (800) GOVERNOR!

How can you concoct a successful story of your own? Read on.

SEVENTEEN

HOOK 'EM

Fame is a constant effort.
JULES RENARD (1864–1910), FRENCH NOVELIST, PLAYWRIGHT

1. Give reporters a dream story.
2. Uncover all the angles.
3. Package your information in a catchy way.

Michael Webb of Cary, North Carolina, is editor and publisher of The RoMANtic, a newsletter that contains hundreds of tips for fun and creative romance. Webb has at least ten thousand subscribers, has been featured in numerous media outlets, and has syndicated a romance column in fifty publications, both print and electronic. How did he get such exposure? When he first started, he sent press releases to 150 newspapers and magazines, whose addresses he found in a media guide at his public library. In the first year, he was written up in a number of newspapers, but no magazines. Eventually the news wire services picked up the stories

175

and sent them to their subscribers. That's when the magazines took notice of The RoMANtic.

Today, Webb sends press releases on Valentine's Day. And when he doesn't have a reason to contact the media, he invents one. For example, he once sent out a release that said, "North Carolina Couple Celebrates 95th Wedding Anniversary." Then he explained that he and his wife celebrate their anniversary every *month*—ninety-five and counting when the release went out.

Webb also created National Resurrect Romance Week in August, which he advertised in *Chase's Calendar of Events*. Radio DJs on the lookout for an interesting interview have frequently contacted Webb to discuss the holiday, and ask him for romance tips.

How has he reaped such great publicity?

"It's like planting a thousand seeds out there," Webb explains. "You have to keep throwing them out there and throwing them out there and throwing them out there and before you know it, they start to germinate."

What Webb has done is quite simple: He has found a way to create news hooks that lure editors, and eventually get them to bite on a story.

You can too. Here's how.

1. GIVE REPORTERS A DREAM STORY.

Christian LesStrang knew he had a winner on his hands. His mother, author Barbara LesStrang, had invented the ideal deterrent to carjacking: Safe-T-Man, a life-sized, realistic-looking man that could be inflated and placed in the front seat of a car. This personal safety device was the result of LesStrang's research, which showed that most carjackers tend to target drivers who are alone, and therefore more vulnerable.

Christian's first marketing tactic, in 1994, was a proactive media campaign to concentrate on Safe-T-Man's uniqueness. "It's the best thing we ever did," says the twenty-five-year-old whiz kid. "We came along with a life-sized, simulated male companion created by a mother in her sixties with seven kids, who was a best-selling author. It's a reporter's dream."

He was right. Since launched in 1994, "we've had more than six million dollars in free publicity and three hundred media appearances," says Christian. Safe-T-Man's list of media placements fills at least ten pages—in small type!

The marketing efforts began by sending out press releases to print and broadcast outlets in the country's top twenty-five crime areas. The product had a broad appeal, says Christian, as it had numerous angles including human-interest, crime, and even some humor. "Before you knew it, Safe-T-Man appeared on *Geraldo*, which brought one thousand phone calls and two hundred and fifty orders in the next twenty-four hours," Christian adds. At last count, Safe-T-Man had made it into catalogs such as Sky Mall and The Sharper Image, and even into the feature film *Forget Paris* starring Billy Crystal, and the *Ellen* TV show.

ONE THING LEADS TO ANOTHER.

Safe-T-Man's press materials also included phone numbers for crime statistics and information on how to avoid carjackings, making it a "public service" hook as well.

2. UNCOVER ALL THE ANGLES.

What's the bait that will reel in an editor or TV producer? Try these hooks on for size.

NEW, UNPRECEDENTED

Is your product or service the leader of the pack? This hook would include stories on new cures for cancer, new products for nail-biters, and electric cars on the market. A few years ago, a small Massachusetts bank reaped tons of publicity when it

Points to remember:

- Your story must interest the media outlet's audience—so make sure you know who its audience is.
- Look for the news value in your story.
- Don't confuse a news story with an advertisement.

held an unprecedented "Senior Prom" for its clients sixty-five years old and older.

BREAKING NEWS

Be ready to pounce. If you can link you or your business to breaking news, call the media—quick! If the Rolling Stones announce they're breaking up, and a crowd of mourners dressed in black holds an impromptu vigil in the "R" section of your music store, pick up the phone! You can bet that the next two people through your doors will be a news photographer and reporter.

TREND

Does your story tap into a social, political, or economic trend? The media probably won't care about your restaurant's new children's menu, but they will be interested to hear about your innovative Monday night babysitting service for patrons. Especially if you pitch your business as an example of an evolving trend toward "family-friendly" businesses. Please note that it takes three or more to create a trend, so if you use this hook, supply the reporter with names of other businesses doing something similar. To avoid giving your competition publicity, look for businesses outside your field or geographical area—say, a furniture store with a play area, a beauty salon with children's videotapes, or a restaurant in a different city that also offers babysitting.

The launch of unisex fragrances such as CK One was another trend story. So was the new ManUndercover Collection from Nancy Ganz, which was launched in 1996 and capitalized on the newfound vanity of men. Ganz, who had invented the HipSlip and basically resurrected the woman's girdle, simply extended her line to include men. She gave each clothing item a clever name, such as Double Agent boxer shorts, to tie in with the recently released James Bond movie, and touted them as ideal for guys with "guts."

Remember the Dacyczyns? Their *Tightwad Gazette* succeeded partly because it hitched itself onto the national trend
of most consumers to cut back and save money during the
recession.

In Washington, D.C., Mary Naylor capitalized on a national
trend: the need of consumers for personal service. In 1987 she
launched Capitol Concierge, a business that sets up concierges in
office-building lobbies, supplying everything from catered
lunches to dry cleaning pick up, travel arrangements, and flower
delivery. Naylor's timeliness, especially in the area of one-to-one
marketing, landed her a feature story in the October 1995 issue
of *Inc.* magazine.

California entrepreneur Julie Sautter hooked into *two*
national trends in 1994, during the craze for WonderBra push-up
bras and the heightened fears about silicone breast implants. Her
new product was Curves—lifelike, silicone-gel breast enhancers
that are worn over the breasts and inside a bra; they're even as
bouncy as the real things. "Silicone is so great, I figured, 'Why not
put it on the *outside* of the breast?'" Sautter says.
Sautter, who had a background in marketing, gave a
few free samples to TV stars and costume designers.
Her ploy worked; today, scores of soap-opera stars and
supermodels secretly wear Curves, including actresses
on *Baywatch*. "We tried to position ourselves to
become newsworthy," says Sautter, who also got her
product on an *Oprah* show that focused on celebrity
beauty secrets.

Points to remember:

- Piggyback on more than one trend, if possible.
- Give away free samples.
- Let it snowball.

ANTI-TREND

On the flip side, has your business bucked a trend? A thriving
privately owned pharmacy or hardware store in a region domi-
nated by chain stores is certainly newsworthy. Jolt highly caf-
feinated cola was an anti-trend story, launched at a time when
people were moving to caffeine-free beverages.

OFFBEAT

Does your business have an unusual angle? An editor of the now-defunct *New York Sun* described newsworthiness this way: "If a dog bites a man, it's not news. If a man bites a dog, it's news." When Oprah Winfrey did a beauty show about unusual products for women, she discussed Bag Balm, a Vermont-made salve that prevents chapped cows udders. It gave the Vermont company unparalleled publicity. A Connecticut car wash got almost a full-page of coverage in the *Boston Globe* when it was revealed that it instituted free fifteen-minute massages by qualified therapists to drum up business.

Robert Shillman, Ph.D., is president of Cognex Corporation in Natick, Massachusetts, a pioneer in machine-vision systems—basically, computers that can see. Shillman claims that Cognex was the first company to include a hologram on its annual report, and among the first to be a nonsmoker and nonsmoking company, which generated great press coverage. All of the employees—called Cognoids—are trained in the "Cognex salute," adapted from the Three Stooges.

"The media is drawn by our management style," says Shillman. "They make for outlandish stories. We're happy to be profiled in other sections of the newspaper and media besides the business sections."

The first story ever written about the company, Shillman says, was in *Venture* and it featured Shillman as its centerfold. Another story, in the *Boston Globe*, showed Shillman lying in a bar in a Boston restaurant with the headline, "He Did It His Way"; the story referred to Shillman's business trips to Japan, where the residents have a love of both karaoke and the Sinatra song, "My Way."

SIGNIFICANT

Are you doing something that affects people in a profound way? A research lab may employ a dozen or more people, but if it discovers a cure for cancer, you can bet it will make headlines.

TIMELY

Can you peg your story to a current event? During the O. J. Simpson trial, a manufacturer of back friendly chairs was profiled in both the *Boston Globe* and the *Boston Herald* after Judge Ito ordered an ergonomically friendly "BackSaver" chair for himself in the courtroom. Whenever the cameras focused on Ito, they also unwittingly focused on the chair. Had Ito ordered it during any other time, the media probably wouldn't have cared. Don't forget about seasonality; here's where you'd promote the tenth anniversary of your business, summer hairdos by your salon for the June issues of fashion magazines, and autumn bouquets for the October wedding pages.

CELEBRITY ENDORSEMENT

Can you link your service or product to a well known person? Steve Latour, "The Lei Man," has delivered gratis goods and "leid" a wealth of luminaries, including President Clinton and Harry Connick Jr., which invariably gets mentioned in the press.

SUPERLATIVE

Is your service or product the biggest? Smallest? The last? In summer, drive-in movie theaters are a frequent news story, simply because there are so few of them left. Tanya and Matt's Ice Cream, a scoop shop in Tampa, Florida, generates great publicity every July—National Ice Cream Month—by creating Florida's largest ice-cream cone, and simultaneously holding an ice-cream eating contest.

SLICE OF LIFE

Fiske's General Store in Holliston, Massachusetts, called the local newspaper when they received a shipment of Beanie Babies, the wildly popular McDonald's promotion. Similarly, a limousine driver could invite a reporter to drive along with him on prom night. Or an accountant could invite a reporter to spend a day at the office on April 14—the day before tax deadline.

Likewise, a convenience-store owner might extend an invitation to a reporter to observe the goings-on with the lottery machine when the jackpot reaches higher-than-ever sums.

LOCAL

Do you do something that matters to people in your area? The grand opening of a gift shop that's opening in struggling downtown Jonesville isn't going to make it into the *New York Times*. However, it may appear in the *Jonesville Daily News*, especially if the opening is tied into a broader story about downtown revitalization.

Debbie Hobar, founder of Precious Places, a shop-at-home children's room decorating service in Fairfax Station, Virginia, used tactics that succeeded in getting Precious Places mentioned in *Glamour*, *Entrepreneur*, and *Home Office Computing*. "As soon as you're in one national publication, it snowballs," says Hobar, who received some two hundred calls per day after the exposure. "As soon as you hit a national publication, your business takes a whole new approach," Hobar says. "The key is to be prepared to have that kind of exposure because what could be very beneficial may be detrimental."

BE READY WHEN THE MEDIA CALLS!

COMMUNITY INVOLVEMENT

As you saw in the chapter on Civic Marketing, civic-minded businesses frequently gain the attention of the media. Steve Belkin, founder of Trans National Group, for example, gets written up in the newspapers every year when he charters a private jet and takes Boston journalists, celebrities, politicians—and average, everyday Joes—to the Holocaust Museum in Washington, D.C., for a day to foster goodwill and understanding between people.

HUMAN INTEREST

Do you, one of your employees, or even a customer, have an interesting tale to tell? The expansion of a tailor's shop isn't likely to receive press attention—unless the owner is a Vietnamese refugee who braved a treacherous ocean crossing, learned a new language, and worked eighteen-hour days to become successful. People make a story come alive. The best stories are injected with a human element.

EXPERTISE

Sometimes the best publicity comes about when you're simply quoted in a story because of your expertise or affiliation. If you've written a newsletter or book, make sure to send it to the media, which is always looking for story ideas. Many of the obligatory guest experts on talk shows are there because they've been published.

Debbie Hobar of Precious Places, frequently generates publicity by positioning herself as an expert on children. "I send a media kit to the local news stations during the back-to-school season, or Child Safety Month," says Hobar. "These are different events that the Juvenile industry recognizes throughout the year."

MILESTONE/ANNIVERSARY

Local newspapers frequently run items about employee promotions and when companies reach important milestones. Entrepreneur Marci Blaze remarks that she once worked at a public-relations agency that was retained by Nabisco to generate publicity for the 100th anniversary of the sandwich cookie. "It was difficult to make this newsworthy with a really limited budget," she says. However, it was around that time that the movie *Jaws* was released, and Universal hosted a "Jaws Big Mouth" contest. Blaze got a brainstorm: She approached Nabisco and got them to bake the biggest Fig Newton ever, to give to the contest winner. A photo of it wound up running in UPI.

CREATE AN UNUSUAL PHOTO OPPORTUNITY.

CONTROVERSY

Barry Potekin, the founder of Chicago's Gold Coast Dogs restaurant, created a brilliant marketing ploy that translated into thousands of dollars. Potekin wanted Gold Coast Dogs to be the Number One vendor of hot dogs and hamburgers—even though Nathan's was reportedly moving into town. So, spoofing the famous beer wars of the 1930s, Potekin wrote a press release announcing Chicago's "hot dog wars" and included references to Al Capone and the New York hot dogs "crossing state lines." After sending his press release to local and national media, Potekin almost immediately got a phone call from Connie Chung. From there, the coverage offered "insane publicity," says Potekin. "I got a million dollars of PR out of it.... I singlehandedly chased Nathan's out of Chicago."

Other angles to consider:

- Unique
- Important
- Interesting
- Huge success/Award
- Provocative
- Informative
- Improved
- Special event

When you're unsure about angles for your business, go through your local newspaper and try to determine which "hook" was used for each story; chances are, you may come up with a few zingers you wouldn't have ordinarily thought of! Make sure to look at your business with a fresh eye; it's a great way to discover news value.

READ THE PAPER; WATCH THE NEWS.

Put yourself in the shoes of the media: Why would their audience care about your story? What's in it for their readers? Then spin your story in that direction.

FOLLOW IN THE MEDIA'S FOOTSTEPS.

You should ask yourself: What draws me to a particular story? What do my clients, prospects, and peers watch/read/listen to? What is the human side or the personal story that goes with my service/product?

You probably know the answer; after all, your many years spent watching TV, listening to the radio, and reading newspapers and magazines have already made you something of a media expert, and given you an idea of what's newsworthy.

ASK YOURSELF A QUESTION.

Remember: the media needs a compelling reason to write about your business—just as your customers need a compelling reason to buy your product or service. The media wants to service their readers with information, education, inspiration, and entertainment. If you can walk your walk, and talk your talk— then you can dance this dance.

3. PACKAGE YOUR INFORMATION IN A CATCHY WAY.

After you identify your new/unique/provocative/offbeat angle, you must *package* your story idea to the press in the most clever, appealing way possible. Remember: Print editors and broadcast assignment editors are bombarded with information every day; they receive hundreds of phone calls, faxes, invitations, and press kits. Your mission—if you choose to accept it—is to make your pitch stand out from the crowd. The best press releases and press kits are those that have style and substance—a catchy, ingenious, attention-getting twist that sparks media interest about a news-worthy story. These are the press releases and press kits that create the phone calls that get answered!

EVERYONE'S DOING A BRAND-NEW DANCE NOW . . .

However, occasionally something so newsworthy happens that you won't need any gimmick whatsoever. If the President of the United States decides to visit your company, the story is so inherently newsworthy that you won't have to worry about buying red, white, and blue envelopes. But, until then, you may want to consider creative tactics.

IF THE SHOE FITS, WRAP IT UP IN A SHOE BOX...

Points to remember:

- Treat the media in the same way you would treat a client or customer.
- Remember—you are a source, not an advertiser.
- The easier you make a reporter's or editor's job, the more willing they will be to work with you in the present—and the future.

Debbi Karpowicz, co-author of this book, imple-mented clever packaging when she wrote *I Love Men in Tasseled Loafers*, a humorous dating book on how to judge men by their shoes. (The book was newsworthy because its humorous premise was entertaining and provocative. It also tapped into the trend at that time for books about being single.) Karpowicz used a wealth of shoe-related themes to help her promote her book; it sold in shoe stores and in the shoe department at Nordstrom—not just in bookstores. She had a spe-cial drink created, the "Tasseled Loafer," which was served at her book-signing parties at hotels. Recipe cards were also printed up and handed out. The celebrations also included music such as "Blue Suede Shoes" and "Footloose." The hotels also gave Karpowicz their room amenities of shoehorns and shoe bags. Karpowicz took her book, the recipe cards, the shoehorns and bags, and sent them to the media in shoe boxes that were provided to her by the Allen-Edmonds Shoe Company. She also wrote a press release, rolled it up, and tied it with the actual leather laces and tassels that Allen-Edmonds provided. Karpowicz also concocted chocolate loafer lollipops, and included them in her press kit.

Points to remember:
- Package it in a witty way.
- Get complementary businesses to back your promotion.
- Use every angle.

In response, Karpowicz received scores of calls from curious local and national print and broadcast media; editors almost unanimously proclaimed that her presentation was one of the wittiest that they had ever seen. (Even Boston University, Karpowicz's alma mater, used her press kit as a case study in public-relations classes, while the Authors Guild and the National Writers Union sought her out as a guest speaker on how to market books to the media.) Karpowicz, her book, and the drink were profiled by beverage journals; footwear trade publications; and in the book-review, fashion, and lifestyle pages of national newspapers. She also became something of a dating expert in the process and made numerous TV and radio appearances on the subject, in addition to auditioning for *The Dating Game*. She also got the footwear company Pappagallo to provide her with complimentary shoes, which she wore and promoted at all of her media appearances.

The result of her efforts? *I Love Men in Tasseled Loafers* was covered by more than one hundred print and broadcast media.

Karpowicz also has done other things to successfully obtain a response from the media. Once, when trying to reach Helen Gurley Brown of *Cosmopolitan* magazine, Karpowicz wrote her a letter and enclosed diet dessert gelatin and raisins. She chose those two items because she had just read Brown's book, *Having It All*, in which the New York publisher described her penchant for those two foods. Karpowicz got her reply within a week. Likewise, when Karpowicz hoped to contact the editor of *Boston* magazine, she wrote a letter and enclosed two of his favorite cigars, which had just been mentioned in an article about him in the *Boston Globe*. She sent her package on Saturday and got a response from him on Monday morning.

DO YOUR HOMEWORK.

Debbie Hobar of Precious Places got the media's interest with one clever device that succinctly told the story about her children's decorating service. In Hobar's media kits, she included pieces of a children's puzzle and the message, "Decorating a child's room can be a puzzling experience for most parents—but Precious Places helps to put the pieces of the puzzle together." Says Hobar: "I try to do things that are unique to children and the service that I provide."

Loriann Hoff Oberlin is yet another writer who found a unique angle for herself. The author of *Writing for Money*, Oberlin purchased pens containing shredded money, which she sent out to the media with copies of her book. "People still remember what my package is when I remind them about the pens," she says.

Oberlin pitched the ideas in her book as a way for women, retirees, college students, and graduates to earn extra money. "Any self-employed person needs to be creative and look beyond the obvious," Oberlin says. "Look at other options besides selling in bookstores."

SEND ITEMS RELATED TO YOUR MESSAGE.

SEND AN ATTENTION-GETTING TELEGRAM

Tiffany James, the president of UndercoverWear in Tewksbury, Massachusetts, definitely danced to a different drummer to get on *Donahue*. James, who founded her multimillion-dollar lingerie company in 1978, has made scores of TV appearances. But a few years ago, she sought to speak on the one show that hadn't yet booked her: *Donahue*. "I tried for six to eight months to get on the show," James says, but to no avail. Then she got a brainstorm. On the day that the show *Evening Magazine* was to feature UndercoverWear, James, who at this point had Donahue's home address, *sent* him an unsigned telegram that simply said, "Watch *Evening Magazine* tonight." The next day the show's producer called and offered James a slot on the program.

Did James say yes? Not exactly. For one thing, the producer offered her a thirteen-minute segment. No, said James, who insisted that she needed an entire hour to tell the UndercoverWear story. Even when offered a half-hour, James insisted on sixty minutes. Not only did she get her wish of an entire hour devoted to UndercoverWear, using the models that she preferred, James also got the show to pay for her to fly first-class to Chicago.

Then James took yet another tactic (and kids, don't try this at home unless you're really confident): because she wanted to make the very best impression on her host, James had her hair cut in a flip with bangs, so her hairdo resembled that of Marlo Thomas, Donahue's wife. This ploy was James's psychological way, she says, of winning over the TV host. And she did—in her own, inimitable way.

"That single appearance," explained then-spokeswoman Cynthia Prunty, "was responsible for introducing UndercoverWear lingerie products to millions of people across the nation, and catapulting sales into a multimillion-dollar category.... And women across the country began joining our sales force, all thanks to Phil Donahue!"

Adds James: "'No' isn't in my vocabulary," says the company founder, who was thirty years old when she made her first million

Points to remember:

- Send an unsigned telegram with a direct message.
- Ask for what you want.
- Stay positive—you can't afford the stupidity of a negative thought!

dollars. "I won't allow myself to entertain fears or negative thoughts."

Sometimes all it takes is a very simple strategy. The owners of a Halloween-themed amusement park frequently include surprises with their press invitations. One year they sprinkled tiny plastic spiders in the envelope, so the creatures spilled out when the invitation was opened. Another year they tucked a package of candy corn into the envelope. The owners of a car-restoration business mailed the *Today* show a postcard of themselves standing next to an antique auto; the flip side offered the producer a ride in the car.

After you've devised the winning angles, you're poised to reap oodles of media attention. In Chapter 18, you'll discover other ways to prepare for positive press.

EighteEN

PREPARE FOR POSITIVE PRESS

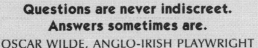

**Questions are never indiscreet.
Answers sometimes are.**
OSCAR WILDE, ANGLO-IRISH PLAYWRIGHT

1. Draft a media list.
2. Write the perfect pitch letter and press kit.
3. Make contact.

Your business needs the media, and the media—with all of that space and airtime to fill—definitely needs you. Furthermore, it wants to know Who, What, Where, Why, and How. Here's how to start a beautiful relationship together.

1. DRAFT A MEDIA LIST.

After determining your newsworthiness, *draft a media list* of reporters and publications that might be interested in your story; don't forget to single out special columns, columnists, reporters, and broadcasters within media outlets, in addition to the business pages. Be sure that all of these names are entered into a software database program such as ACT, Goldmine, TeleMagic, FileMaker Pro, and so on. (Check with your nearest office superstore or computer store to determine the best program for you.) For example, with *I Love Men in Tasseled Loafers,* Karpowicz pitched it not only to hundreds of editors, but to editors in varying beats: Fashion, Lifestyle, Singles, Book Reviews, and even talk shows, *The Dating Game,* and footwear-trade publications.

Request an editorial calendar so you can time your pitch. It's smart to send out press releases on a regular basis—but if you can tie your story angle into a specific "special section" or "three-part series" you'll be way ahead of the game.

Do your homework and start regionally. National publications and broadcast stations receive hundreds of press kits every day, so you're better off going local first, where the editors may be hungrier for good stories and more receptive. Tune into your local TV and radio stations and read your local newspapers. Not only will this exercise offer a wealth of names; it will allow you to familiarize yourself with each media outlet's style and tone, which will help you to modify your message. Another method is to simply call your local TV stations and newspapers to get the correct names of editors covering specific areas. (This is also the time to request a media kit, which contains demographic information, plus an editorial calendar that shows where you might plug your story in.) When you send your pitch letter or press kit to the media in your region, make sure to include on the outside envelope the words, "This story has your local angle." Make sure to correctly spell the reporter's name, and to have the correct address of the media outlet.

BEGIN WITH THE BOY OR GIRL NEXT DOOR.

Keep your list updated; job turnover and job changes tend to be high within the media industry. You don't want to waste time, energy, and postage sending materials to someone who left the job two years ago. Before sending your package, place a brief call to notify the recipient that it's on its way. If you can leave your message on voice mail, all the better.

UPDATE YOUR DATABASE. YOU'RE ONLY AS GOOD AS YOUR LIST.

Always feed your database program with updated media contact information. Don't let it go hungry, because you're only as good as your list.

A visit to the library and books such as *Bacon's Media Directories* can also provide you with more names than you could possibly handle. Remember: It's not the *quantity* of media, it's *quality*. It's better to have ten great media contacts than one hundred that are less-than-wonderful.

Besides the well known mainstream press, it's also wise to *consider alumni publications and newsletters*, which also reach a wide, diversified audience.

Try a newsletter—yours or theirs. Kamal Shariff, founder of Kamite Comics, which focuses on minority superheroes, asked a friend to write a press release for him. As a result, his business has been featured on CNN, the *Boston Globe*, the *Boston Herald*, and on Boston's NBC affiliate. After Shariff was profiled in a NYNEX newsletter in 1995, he received a call from an owner of a software company in Rhode Island who proposed an arrangement to develop a three-part comic-book series called "Numidian Force," as an interactive CD-ROM property. Shariff now derives licensing income as they sell it.

DON'T BE PICKY.

2. WRITE THE PERFECT PITCH LETTER AND PRESS KIT.

This is the letter that is attached to the front of your press kit. Make sure to grab your audience ASAP—you'll only get ten seconds of attention!

- Keep your letter succinct and double-check your spelling—especially the name of the journalist or producer.
- Begin your pitch much like the beginning of a news story in a newspaper or on television. Summarize your story by using the editorial "inverted pyramid" that starts with the most important information, ends with the least important, and answers who, what, when, where, why, and how.
- Use statistics and be specific instead of making unsubstantiated claims like "business is great." Details make the difference.
- Provide a direct and personal benefit of your idea. The media is interested in discovering how something in particular has affected someone. Explain and include a personal story.
- Is there a larger issue, which you can "wrap" your story around?
- Customize each letter, especially if you are sending out more than one. People like to be addressed by name rather than "Dear Editor."
- Tell each person you're writing to when you will follow up—then do so.
- Proofread each letter, and ask a friend to read it for clarity, content, and errors. You might not have a second chance to make a positive first impression!

DO THE WRITE THING!

- Use your own letterhead, especially if you have received outside help. Editors are hesitant to follow up with someone who's not directly involved in the press release.
- Stick to the format shown. A press release should always have a date. This implies that it is time-sensitive and therefore, news.
- Include a contact name and phone number. Make sure that person can provide complete and accurate information, as well as line up interviews and take that extra step. When you include a contact person other than yourself, your business appears to be more successful and professional. If

you don't have one, make one up! It will instantly alert you when the press calls for more information, and you have the option of taking a message or identifying yourself on the phone. (Don't worry; smaller publications do this all the time. When a handful of staff writes most of the articles, they sometimes also use pseudonyms in addition to their real names, to make the publication appear bigger.)

- Keep your press release to one page, two at most. If it is two pages, type "more" at the bottom of the first page. Double-space and use 1- or 1.5-inch margins. At the top of the second page, type your slug line (a brief summary of the story's contents) followed by a dash and a page number. (End your release by typing "-30-," "###," or the word "END.")

- The headline should read like that of a news story; don't put your company name in the headline. "Local Employer Lets Workers Sleep It Off" is better than "Software Systems Inc. Institutes Daily Naptime for Employees."

- Be as direct and succinct as possible. Use the inverted-pyramid style of reporting that begins with the most important information first. Make your best points in the first couple of sentences.

- Use quotes from yourself, your company spokesperson, industry insiders, employees, customers, and clients who can help support your position. If others can't come up with a good quote, make them up—and simply get their approval.

- Be honest in your presentation of your product or service.

- Emphasize the *benefits* of your product or service—not just the features.

- Customize your press release to your audience. Talk shows look for different stories than CNBC.

Then, *craft your press kit*—an information packet all about your business, including press releases.

To reiterate, simply buy two-pocket, 8-by-10-inch folders, into which you place:

- Press releases
- Photocopies of articles that have been written about you, which lend you credibility but offer the recipient ideas about new ways you can be covered. (But don't send clips from one competitor to another. In other words, the *Today* show won't consider your segment if it aired on *Good Morning America* a week earlier.)
- Photocopies of awards your business has won
- Brochures and other collateral materials
- Photographs with identifying labels attached to the back; most newspapers prefer black-and-white glossies over color photos. (See pp. 209 and 210 for names of companies that reprint photographs in quantity.)

The front cover of the press-kit folder is reserved for your pitch letter. Have a strong first paragraph in your pitch letter and a catchy headline in your press release. If you don't have enough material for a press kit, a simple pitch letter will do.

Also consider including:

- A fact sheet about your business/industry
- A bio of you (or your upper management)
- Answers to commonly asked questions about your business
- Samples of your product (This is very important. All journalists need to see, touch, taste, and feel your product.)
- An invitation to your factory/hotel/special event
- Rolodex cards printed with your business name, address, phone number, and fax (It helps to make the identifying top portion in a bright color, and your industry. Often, editors file sources by their specialty, and not by the actual company name.)
- A sheet listing various angles in which you could gain editorial coverage

A few words about this last point. You can greatly help editors when you include a separate list of story angles into which your business can fit. The angle of your story can also make—or break—a reporter's interest. Let's suppose your restaurant has a novel theme to it—say, it's outfitted with cars and used-car parts. You might suggest that your restaurant tie into the national trend of theme restaurants such as the Fashion Cafe or Hard Rock Cafe. Or, you might suggest an offbeat story about the difficulties of finding quality car parts to decorate with. Or you might propose that the reporter write a first-person, humorous story about being a waitperson for a day. Or you might propose a story on National Restaurant Day, or Car Week, if such things exist. (Read *Chase's Book of Annual Events* for details.) Try to add statistics whenever you can. There are usually several angles for any one story. Don't get stuck into thinking that a "story" means a full-blown business feature just on your company!

THE WALTZ, TANGO, OR CHA-CHA?

It also helps when you actually think from the reporter's point of view. Remember: In most—but not all—cases, a reporter will interview several sources for one story. So, it will actually benefit you if you mention businesses that complement, and in some cases, compete with your business. Providing reporters with this type of information will help them write a better, more interesting, well-rounded story—which is always your goal! Don't fool yourself into believing that a news story on your business will be a commercial. It won't. In fact, the more you can offer names of competitors doing the same thing in your industry, the better. Think of yourself as a source, not an advertiser.

IF I WERE IN HIS SHOES . . .

You may also want to *subscribe to an electronic or print clipping service*. It will send you tearsheets of relevant newspaper and magazine articles, or transcripts of TV and radio segments. (See p. 214 for more information.)

HOW TO KEEP ABREAST?

DON'T JUST SAY "CHEESE." SAY "BRIE"!

It's smart to *include a professional headshot* in your press kit; these are straight-on portraits taken from the shoulders up. Newspapers often run headshots with their business briefs and sometimes use them with stories when action shots aren't available.

CAPTURE YOURSELF ON FILM.

Your headshot should last about four years, so treat it as an investment. Hire a professional photographer; if you're a woman, use a makeup artist. It's also wise to hire a wardrobe consultant, who can make the most of your appearance. Take Polaroid pictures of yourself in different outfits, to find your ideal "look."

Here's how to make sure you'll click with your photographer:

- Interview your photographer and review his or her portfolio to determine if you'll be a good match.
- Schedule your photo session when you're typically most alert, and make it your priority for that day.
- Get plenty of rest the night before and avoid alcohol, which can make your face puffy.
- Determine the color of the background the photographer will use so that your outfit won't clash.
- Always wear a jacket—it projects authority.
- Men can wear a subtly patterned tie but women should avoid stripes and checks. Keep jewelry to a minimum—and don't wear anything too trendy or funky.

- Avoid bulky fabrics; remember, the camera adds ten pounds!
- Gray, brown, blue, and pastels photograph the best, even in black-and-white.
- If you wear glasses but will be photographed without them, remove them ahead of time so your face is not left with indentations.
- Avoid frosted eye shadows, lip gloss, or any cosmetics that reflect light; stick with creams and mattes. If you're having black-and-white and color photographs during the same sitting, stick with minimal makeup colors and neutral tones.

The "action shot" is yet another photograph you may want to consider for your press kit. But *avoid* what newspaper professionals call "grip and grins"—those cliche shots of:

- People standing in a semicircle holding shovels for a ground-breaking
- One person passing an oversized check to another
- People doing nothing except staring at the camera
- People standing behind microphones
- One person posed before a ribbon with scissors in hand
- Someone holding up his or her product

Most newspapers will not print these photographs; if they pick one, the shot is shrunk to the size of a postage stamp! Be creative!

LIGHTS, CAMERA, ACTION

If your business is visually compelling, produce a video news release or a B-Roll, which allows you to demonstrate your company or product.

A video news release (VNR), the video version of your written press release, is a fully produced story about your business or product that's usually thirty to fifty minutes long. It uses two audio tracks, one for narration, the other for natural sound; that way, the sounds can be separated for use in a news story. For example, a VNR of your snow-vaporizer might include footage of someone laboring with a snow shovel while a voice-over talks about the health risks of traditional snow-removal methods. Next comes a demonstration of your product, shots of the manufacturing process, and interviews with snow-removal experts, the company president, and satisfied customers.

B-Roll is stock footage of your business that includes interviews and on-location video. It uses natural sound with no narration, so video can be used in a news story. A B-Roll of the snow-vaporizer would be similar to a VNR but without the voice-over. B-Roll allows news editors to construct their own story from the footage. (See p. 214 for information on companies that produce these materials.)

3. MAKE CONTACT.

Next, send the information to the person most likely to report on your topic. For instance, a business reporter may not be interested in your restaurant opening—unless you "wrap" the story around new restaurant openings during a recession. However, your story idea may be more appropriate for the features department or the local news section. Make sure to watch the programs and read the publications that you're pitching to; it should help you get an idea of who covers what. If you're unsure, call the media outlet and ask which editor or reporter might be interested in your story idea. You could also visit the library to read media directories such as *Bacon's*, which lists publications, reporters, and their beats.

Make sure to include industry and alumni publications, and send samples of your product, if applicable. And whatever you do, don't blanket a newsroom with your press release. Your information will be much more effective if it's targeted to one or two people within an organization.

THE FOLLOW-UP

After sending out your information...

DO:

- Follow up with a phone call in one to two weeks.
- Ask if you're calling at a good time and whether the reporter/producer is on deadline. If not, ask if they have a minute or two to speak with you. If you call a TV station,

don't contact anchors or reporters five minutes before air-time when everyone is getting ready for the broadcast.

- Perfect your pitch. Editors and assignment editors usually allow about thirty seconds—thirty seconds!—to discuss possible stories with callers. Write out your "script" on paper, if necessary.
- Act professionally.
- Emphasize the results of your product or service, not its features.
- Ask if you can take the reporter out for lunch, or out for coffee, at their convenience to discuss the story. Don't feel offended if they're too busy and decline.

If you don't actually meet face-to-face, you can still develop a relationship by sending the reporter your newsletter, holiday cards, personal notes to congratulate them on receiving an award or for simply writing a story that you enjoyed—you name it. In addition, should you discover that a reporter is an avid Kona coffee drinker or stamp collector, there's nothing wrong with sending a birthday or Yuletide gift, as long as it's not valued at more than twenty-five dollars. (Many media outlets have strict rules about reporters accepting gifts; newspapers are usually stricter than magazines.)

If the reporter turns down your idea, simply ask if there is someone else at their publication/station who might be interested. Don't take "no" as an absolute "no." Chances are, an editor will contact you in the future if a story or a quote from you is needed. Take a long-term approach.

ASK SOMEONE ELSE TO DANCE.

OK! You're ready to get set and go. But how to make sure your interview will attract and excite reporters—and your audience? The next chapter shows you how.

Nineteen

MAKE YOUR INTERVIEW MEMORABLE

> When producers want to know what the public wants, they graph it as curves. When they want to tell the public what to get, they say it in curves.
> MARSHALL McLUHAN (1911–1980),
> CANADIAN COMMUNICATIONS THEORIST

1. Offer pithy quotes and a lively presentation.
2. Tailor yourself for TV.
3. Confront every crisis.

There you are, face-to-face with Ace Reporter. He asks you several questions about your doorknob business but—Yikes!—you stumble, stutter, and almost forget your name.

You'd obviously make a better impression if you said, "My competition calls me the Ivana Trump of doorknobs, because I've taken a mundane household item and made it ultra glamorous and exciting. You should *see* my hot-pink, tasseled number that's now used in luxury apartments!"

Now you're *really* talking.

1. OFFER PITHY QUOTES AND A LIVELY PRESENTATION.

Make sure you're ready, willing, and able if and when the reporter bites at your bait. It's in your best interest to supply reporters with any information they may need, including the names and telephone numbers of industry sources, associations, clients, customers, and complementary businesses, so you can be considered a good source. Good sources frequently get repeat coverage. Be generous with your time and lively with your anecdotes. The difference between being mentioned at the top of a story—and being buried at the bottom—is often a good quote!

When discussing your story with a reporter...

DO:

- Be forthright. Answer the reporter's questions, even the ones you think are irrelevant.
- Make suggestions for photos, or bring your own.
- Simplify. The reporter has to grasp your expertise so it can be relayed to the lay person.
- Offer details. They make a story come alive!
- Provide written materials that the reporter can take back to the newsroom for reference. Your information may even be filed away for future stories.

WHAT TO DO WHEN MIKE WALLACE CALLS

Train your receptionist in how to take calls from the media. Always, always, always get the reporter's name, publication, phone and fax numbers, and e-mail address. Set a policy that all media inquiries be directed to your attention; if you're unavailable, designate a second and third person to take calls. Ask if the reporter is on deadline and when you need to get back to him. Make sure to find out what issue your interview is slated for. Keep at-the-ready a folder or press kit of information that you can immediately fax or send out.

Don't be offended should you discover that places like Dunkin' Donuts and Starbucks will also be mentioned in a story about your coffee shop. Remember: It's in your best interest to tell the reporter about things that could make the story more interesting. For example, if you know that a man in your town recently made it into *The Guinness Book of Records* for his incessant coffee drinking, by all means share that information. Likewise, if you just heard about a new type of coffee bean that's grown in the United States, make sure to share that information with the reporter. He or she will love you for being a "source" and forever be in your debt.

DON'T:

- Use jargon or technical terms.
- Talk too fast if leaving a message on voice mail. State your name and company at the beginning of the message, and at the end, and make sure to give your phone number twice.
- Make a reporter wait.
- Tell a reporter how to write her story.
- Stray too far from the subject. You'll not only bore the reporter, but chances are your valid comments won't make it into print.
- Ask to read a story before it runs. However, you may request that the reporter call you to fact-check information.

2. TAILOR YOURSELF FOR TV.

What if—Gulp!—you're asked for an on-camera interview? Follow these tips, after you take a deep, deep breath.

DO:

- Ask the host or producer, in the pre-interview, what he plans to discuss. Give them a list of questions you'd like to be asked. Be armed with statistics and data.
- Be forthright. Answer the reporter's questions, even the ones that seem irrelevant.
- Create a list of all of the points you'd like to make. Then whittle them down to five-second "sound bites." Practice in front of a mirror.
- Put your sound bites down on index cards so you can refer to them.

- Be prepared for the "zinger" question you hope won't be asked. That's the one question that's sure to be included!
- Continue making your points, even if the interview isn't going in the direction that you prefer. Keep talking!
- Look at the interviewer or other guest who is speaking. At a call-in show, look directly at the camera when answering caller questions unless you've been otherwise directed. Don't look at the monitors—you don't want the camera to catch you smoothing your hair.
- Sit up straight and lean forward in your chair to show involvement and interest.
- Consider the services of a professional makeup artist and hairdresser, to look your best for a TV appearance.
- Get videotapes of your appearance.

DON'T:

- Be late.
- Try to answer questions that are outside of your expertise.
- Be afraid to make an important point when you feel that the interview is winding down.
- Fidget. Keep hands away from your face, hair, and mouth.

WHAT TO WEAR ON TV?

Women should:

- Keep their wardrobe simple and professional looking. Wear a suit (but never black, white, or red) with a contrasting blouse. Keep accessories to a minimum—less is more.
- Avoid busy prints or polka dots, noisy bracelets, and low-cut blouses (unless your name is Madonna).

Men should:

- Wear a dark-colored suit, light-colored shirt, neutral-colored tie with a subdued pattern, and over-the-calf socks.
- Avoid white or striped shirts, jeweled or gold tie tacks, gold chains or distracting jewelry (unless you're Mr. T).

ON THE RADIO

Radio, the most widespread of the media, is the most intimate of the media, and leaves listeners with a sense of personal involvement.

DO:

- Maintain a friendliness in your voice (unless the subject matter dictates otherwise). Your voice and inflection, plus your answers, shape the listeners' image of you.
- Ask the host if you can use his or her first name. If so, use it a few times but don't overdo it.
- Make your answers concise and use colorful anecdotes and examples to illustrate your points.

After any press interview, follow these words of wisdom to make the most of your contact.

DO:

- Send the reporter or host a thank-you note. File their phone number and address so you can update them on new developments in your business.
- Send them your newsletter and press releases.
- Invite the reporter to lunch and pick up the tab. If lunch can't be arranged, try for a brief meeting over coffee. You'll not only show your gratitude, you'll have an opportunity to connect with a reporter on a more personal level. Don't send a pricey gift, which, if accepted, can be regarded as unethical.

3. CONFRONT EVERY CRISIS.

What if you find yourself in a crisis situation? Prepare yourself ahead of time and follow these tips.

- Plan your response. Be proactive and stick to your point; don't get sidelined. Get your points across in the short time that you have.

- Keep your comments brief and to-the-point, especially if you are interviewed on camera. TV and radio sound bites are twenty seconds or less.
- Don't hide the truth. If there is something in your company's background that the reporter is likely to discover through an outside source, volunteer the information. By being open, the media will portray you as such.
- Don't stonewall. A good reporter will get the story whether or not you cooperate.
- Never say "No comment." It makes you appear evasive. If you can't answer a question, give the reason. If you don't know the answer, offer to get the information for the reporter.
- Be wary of making "off-the-record" comments. Avoid saying anything you would hate to be revealed to the public.

Pawnbroker Michael Goldstein knows all about it; after a priceless violin from Boston's Berklee College of Music wound up at his shop, Goldstein coaxed some super publicity out of what could have been a sour note of business. After hearing of the theft and recovery, the *Boston Herald* called Goldstein for an interview. Instead of issuing a flat "No Comment," Goldstein invited the newspaper to take a picture of his staff posing with the recovered violin. By doing so, Goldstein created an opportunity for himself to educate the public about pawnshops. Stolen goods, he explained, almost never turn up at pawnshops, but when they do, a reputable pawnbroker works hand-in-hand with the police department to catch the crook. With his forthrightness and explanation, Goldstein shifted the slant of the media coverage from the theft and recovery of a violin, to a glowing report on his quick and responsible action.

Now that you've mastered the art of securing perfect publicity, the next chapter will explain how to keep 'em calling.

Points to remember:

- Turn a lemon into lemonade.
- Be forthright.
- Take the opportunity to educate the public.

Twenty

KEEP 'EM CALLING

1. Maintain lasting relationships with the press.
2. Publicize your publicity.
3. Hire a publicist, if you can.

Wow! Your new titanium widgets just reaped huge results—a feature article in *USA Today*, a segment on your local newscast, a mention in a trend story in *Newsweek*; and you were also named "Bachelor of the Month" in *Cosmopolitan*. How to keep the good karma coming?

1. MAINTAIN LASTING RELATIONSHIPS WITH THE PRESS.

Congratulations! With your pithy press releases, creative pitch letters, and useful insider's knowledge, your friends at the newspaper and television station have come to regard you as an invaluable source. Pat yourself on the back—you have succeeded in your goal of developing a solid relationship with the press.

Make sure to show your appreciation. But before you offer a reporter your vacation villa in Hawaii, remember that the press views gifts differently than do your clients in the business world. A reporter must scrupulously avoid all appearances of a conflict of interest. One who accepts a pricey gift from a news source risks being regarded as unethical.

The question is, then, how do you thank the media? The answer is to use your own best judgment. It is inappropriate to send an expensive gift to a reporter immediately before or after an interview. You will make a good impression however, if you send a personal note after the story or segment appears. It is also fine to send your press contacts a book or CD you know they would enjoy or an inexpensive gift to mark a special occasion in his or her personal or professional life—say, an engagement or a promotion.

It's also perfectly acceptable to invite a reporter to lunch and to pick up the tab. In fact, inviting a reporter to lunch accomplishes more than a show of gratitude. Breaking bread with someone allows you to connect on a more personal level. Through occasional lunches, you can keep your press contacts informed of what you are doing, and also learn more about their interests. Keep in mind that it may be difficult for a reporter to break away for lunch, especially those at larger publications and television stations. Generally, those at smaller news outlets or trade journals are under less pressure to churn out stories and have the time to spend with their sources. And don't forget about freelancers, who can make their own schedule and may have an extra hour for lunch with you.

Ethical journalists won't be swayed or "bribed" by small tokens of appreciation; rather, they are likely to remember you when they need a source or resource. Developing an ongoing relationship with the press is like planting a seed; if you water it regularly, you just may like what grows out of it.

Don't forget to send updated press releases and information on a regular basis, as well as your newsletter. Better yet, mail information that's unrelated to your business—but which you know would be of interest to the reporter.

Publicity is a never-ending job. It's a way of life. Seize opportunities that pop up as you read the paper or watch television. Your objective obviously is to publicize your business, but the media cares only about giving its audience information that is enlightening, educational, balanced, and interesting. The better you know your media contacts, the better your chances of making news.

GRATITUDE IS THE BEST FORM OF COURTESY.

2. PUBLICIZE YOUR PUBLICITY.

It may seem obvious, but too many small business people receive media coverage—and then let it go. The key is to take your publicity and publicize it!

For starters, there's no reason you can't send out press releases that publicize your recent coverage. If you made an appearance on *Good Morning America*, tell your local newspaper about it! Furthermore, obtain a video copy of your appearance, which you can make duplicates of and send to other producers. You can also place the words "As seen on *Good Morning America*" in your advertising.

If you've received print coverage, make copies of the article and send them to new and potential customers. Frame the article and prominently display it at your place of business.

Reprint the article in your newsletter (with permission from the newspaper or magazine) or in a client's newsletter.

Get the video or cassette tape. If you are a radio or television guest, keep a copy of the broadcast. You can use this to show other producers how well you come across on the air.

Photocopy all of your press clippings onto high-quality white paper, such as glossy or heavy weight stock. Make sure that the publication's masthead and date appear above the story. (You may need to cut and paste.) If the clip is more than two years old, consider blotting out the date. Use these as you would your other marketing materials, and include them in your professional portfolio. You can also reprint them in your annual report, and send them out with future pitches.

Remember—publicity begets more and more publicity. But it's up to you.

3. HIRE A PUBLICIST, IF YOU CAN.

If your pockets are deep enough, or if you simply can't do it all yourself, consider hiring a publicist. When you do, you are buying the publicist's time, expertise, and contacts. Furthermore, when someone else promotes you, it lends you even more credibility, as you are not tooting your own horn. It's always more impressive to have someone else lauding your talents and abilities—especially someone who's paid for their marketing savvy, professional contacts, and media placements.

PUBLICISTS GIVE GOOD PHONE.

To find a publicist, ask your colleagues for referrals. Or, watch the news to discover businesses that always get good press coverage; then call to find out who their publicist is.

Another method is to simply call the publication or media outlet where you seek coverage, and simply ask who they might recommend as a publicist. The Public Relations Society of America and the Publicity Club in your area can also offer referrals. Ask for references from colleagues in your industry, and from your Board of Advisors. (See p. 209 for more information.)

After obtaining several names, conduct interviews to find out whom you feel the most comfortable with. You may be better off with a small firm that charges hourly, rather than a huge PR agency that charges thousands of dollars per month for its services.

A public-relations professional will conduct lengthy interviews with you to obtain information about your company and its goals. Then he or she will whittle all of that down to numerous press releases, and compile a list of media to be contacted. Remember, a public-relations pro can't guarantee anything; all one can do is send out the information and get your business name in front of the media on a regular basis. If those efforts are made, there's a good chance that your business will be covered; If they're *not*, you're almost sure not to!

You can help your PR person by constantly feeding them new and interesting information. Did a celebrity visit the hair salon today? Have you recently handed out a scholarship? Did your chocolate bagel receive an award? Make sure to call the PR pro—pronto!

DO:

- Offer free samples of your product to give media people a "hands-on" experience of it.
- Keep your media contacts on a Rolodex or database for easy access when you get a new client, invent a new product, offer a unique service, or accomplish something newsworthy.
- Send new information about your idea or business to press contacts who have written about you in the past.
- Write a brief note thanking the person who interviewed you and/or produced the program.

- Maintain an updated media file of special sections and segments where your idea might fit in.
- Make photocopies of all the stories published about your business, or which use you as a source for quotes.

DON'T:

- Delay sending information about yourself or your new business to the media—especially if they call you to request it. Build your credibility with first-class follow-through and a commitment to assist them in their jobs.
- Take a reporter's directness or curtness as a personal assault. Remember, they are continuously approached by individuals and companies vying for valuable space in their media.

Points to remember:

- A publicist has the time and expertise to devote to the pursuit of publicity.
- Work in partnership with your publicist.
- Publicity is a never-ending job.

At this point, you should be fully armed with more than enough marketing ideas and resources to go forth and prosper. From creating your look on paper, to forming strategic alliances, becoming an authority in your field, becoming a personality in your promotional efforts, employing zany and effective marketing, using Civic Marketing, and dealing with the press—now you've really got what it takes.

In fact, now you may even have more ideas than you ever bargained for, which brings us to the last point—one final "P" that can make or break your business:

Persist! Persist! Persist!

PART SIX RESOURCES:

ADVERTISING OPPORTUNITIES FOR EXPERTS AND AUTHORITIES
Radio-TV Interview Report
Bradley Communications
Box 1206
Landsdowne, PA 19050
(800) 989-1400
Fax: (610) 284-3704
You can place advertisements for yourself and your business for distribution to all talk/radio show producers and hosts. Prices vary depending on size and frequency.

Yearbook of Experts, Authorities & Spokespersons
Broadcast Interview Source
2233 Wisconsin Ave. NW
Washington, D.C. 20007-4104
(800) 995-0311
Contact: Mitchell P. Davis, Editor
Place ads for yourself and your business to be distributed to media. Prices vary depending on ad size.

BOOKS
How to Keep Your Press Release Out of the Wastebasket
by Holland Cooke
P.O. Box 1323
Block Island, RI 02807
$12.50 + $2 shipping

6 Steps to Free Publicity
by Marcia Yudkin
Plume-Penguin, $9.95
Available in bookstores or by calling Yudkin directly at (781) 647-9657.

BROADCAST MONITORING AND CLIPPING SERVICES
Clipping services review thousands of daily newspapers and magazines to see

if your company is mentioned. They also provide copies of these articles or audio/videotapes of your coverage, as well as reports that demonstrate the effectiveness of your publicity campaign.

Bacon's Information Inc.
332 S. Michigan Ave.
Chicago, IL 60604
(800) 621-0561
Fax: (312) 922-3127

Burrelle's Press Clipping Service
75 E. Northfield Rd.
Livingston, NJ 07039
(800) US MEDIA (876-3342)
Fax: (973) 992-7675

Corporate Media Services
530 Bunkerhill Rd.
Auburn, NH 03032
(800) 528-1551
Television news monitoring, local and network news and specials. Boston and New Hampshire markets only.

Luce Press Clippings
42 S. Center
Mesa, AZ 85210
(800) 528-8226
Fax: (602) 834-3821

Video Monitoring Services
330 W. 42nd St.
New York, NY 10036
(800) 867-2002
(212) 736-2010
Fax: (212) 268-0761

CAMERA-READY RELEASES/ART
Generate camera-ready matte releases for newspaper and broadcast placements.

NAPS (North America Precis Syndicate)
405 Lexington Ave., Floor 59
New York, NY 10074
(212) 867-9000
Fax: (212) 867-9010

News USA
777 Leesburg Pike, Suite 307 South
Falls Church, Va 22043
(703) 734-6300
Fax: (703) 734-6320

MEDIA DIRECTORIES
Bacon's Directories
(800) 621-0561
Website:
www.BACONSINFO.com
Includes those for magazines, newspapers, radio, health, business, as well as media calendars. All are updated annually, and are also available on CD-ROM. Available at most public libraries; each directory costs about $285.

Boston University Media Guidebook
Boston University Public Relations Dept.
25 Buick St.
Boston, MA 02215
(617) 353-3664
Updated monthly; this guidebook includes tons of information about every media source in New England: dailies, weeklies, cable TV, regular TV, etc., as well as national affiliates. The cost is $450 for profit organizations; renewals are $300 each. Not-for-profits receive 15 percent off both prices.

Burrelle's Media Directory
75 E. Northfield Rd.
Livingston, NJ 07039
(800) 876-3342
Directories available for the entire country and individual states.

Editor and Publisher International Yearbook
(212) 675-4380
Listing of print media, updated annually, $115. Available at most public libraries.

PORTFOLIO RESOURCES
ABC Pictures
1867 E. Florida St.
Springfield, MO 65803-4583
(417) 869-9433
High-quality lithographic prints that cost less to produce than standard photographs. These are ideal for inclusion in press kits and packages, although they are not suitable for reprinting in newspapers.

Mass Photo Co.
1315 Waugh Dr.
Houston, TX 77019
(800) 306-7883
Mass-produced photos made from your original photo, artwork, negative, or transparency. Use for news releases, new product introductions, sales promotions, and other publicity.

NRS Photos
(800) 972-8108
Produces high-quality lithographic prints, and those suitable for newspapers.

PRESS RELEASE DISTRIBUTION
Media Distribution Service (MDS)
70 Finnell Dr.
Weymouth, MA 02188-1124
(781) 337-8964
Fax: (781) 335-3676

PR Newswire
111 Devonshire St., Suite 720
Boston, MA 02109
(617) 482-5355
(Also at 810 Seventh Ave., New York,
NY 10019, [888] 776-3977)

U.S. Newswire
National Press Building, #1272
Washington, D.C. 20045
(202) 347-2770
Fax: (202) 347-2767

PREWRITTEN RELEASES
Package Publicity Service
158 W. 27th St., Suite 908
New York, NY 10001
(212) 255-2872
Fax: (212) 255-2874

PROFESSIONAL ASSOCIATIONS
American Marketing Association
311 S. Wacker Dr., Suite 5800
Chicago, IL 60606
(800) 262-1150

Public Relations Society of America
33 Irving Place
New York, NY 10033
(212) 995-2230

Public Relations Society of America
150 Fifth Ave., #840
New York, NY 10011
(212) 228-7228

Publicity Club of New England
P.O. Box 142
Needham, MA 02192
(617) 742-2524

PR NEWSLETTERS
Each of these newsletters puts public-
relations practitioners in touch with
the needs of editors and broadcasters.

By subscribing, you get specific information on stories that reporters and
producers are looking for. These publications are also helpful if you want to
write about a topic and need additional resources. Fax a clearly written
request for information on your subject matter for an article or report that
you are writing, for example, and wait
for the responses!

Bulldog Reporter
5900 Hollis St., Suite R2
Emeryville, CA 94608-2008
(510) 596-9300
Fax: (510) 596-9331

Contacts Newsletter
500 Executive Blvd., Suite 200
Ossining, NY 10562
(914) 923-9400
Fax: (914) 923-9484

Jack O'Dwyer's Newsletter
271 Madison Ave.
New York, NY 10016
(212) 679-2471
Fax: (212) 683-2750

Communications Resource
6 S. Addison St.
Bensenville, IL 60106
(630) 860-1661
Fax: (630) 860-1672

Partyline
35 Sutton Place
New York, NY 10022
(212) 755-3487
Fax: (212) 755-4859

PR News
1201 Seven Locks Rd., #300
Potomac, MD 20854
(301) 340-2100

PR Reporter
P.O. Box 600
Exeter, NH 03833
(603) 778-0514
Fax: (603) 778-1741

SATELLITE MEDIA TOURS
Produce broadcast materials including radio and video news releases and B-Rolls, and arrange satellite media and radio tours.

Auritt Communications Group
Satellite Media Tours
729 Seventh Ave., 15th Floor
New York, NY 10019
(212) 302-6230
Fax: (212) 302-2969

MediaLink
708 Third Ave., 9th Floor
New York, NY 10017
(212) 682-8300
Fax: (212) 681-2580

News/Broadcast Network
425 Main St.
Ridgefield, CT 06877
(203) 431-6699

GLOSSARY OF TERMS

Action shot A photograph that isn't posed.

Article reprint/Clip A story clipped from a newspaper or magazine or taken from a broadcast.

Attribution The source of information in a story.

Background Information to help a reporter understand the circumstances surrounding a story, but which is not necessarily attributed directly to its source.

Beat A reporter's area of coverage.

B-Roll Stock videotape footage of your business (without narration) that can be sent to broadcast stations.

Byline A line at the beginning of a news story, magazine article, or book, which gives the author's name.

Feature Story emphasizing the human side of the story.

Ghostwriter Someone who will write for you, without taking credit.

Headshot A posed photograph that shows little more than the subject's head and shoulders.

Infomercial An extended commercial format that promotes a product and its use.

Lead The first paragraph of a story, which draws the reader in.

Localize To emphasize the local angle of a story.

Logo A distinctive company signature or trademark.

Masthead The title of a newspaper or periodical as it appears across the first page or front cover. (In magazines, it also lists the publication's staff.)

Niche market A specialized market.

Off-the-record Information given to the reporter with the understanding that it will not be attributed to the source.

Press release A publicity handout given to the media.

Pro bono Donating legal work especially for the public good.

Publicist Someone who publicizes—e.g., a press or literary agent.

Query letter A letter that proposes the story you wish to write and the reason you are an ideal person to write it.

Syndicator An organization selling articles or features to many newspapers, TV and radio stations.

Tag line A brief, attention-getting phrase used in advertising or promotion.

Video news release (VNR) A fully produced, ready-for-broadcast video news story about your company or product.

INDEX

A
Accentuation of expertise, 79–85
Action shot, 218
  in press kit, 199
Address, projecting image
  through, 28–29
Advertising
  appearing in own, 87–90
  making memorable, 121–126
  mentioning your contribu-
    tions in, 162
  paying for, 167–174
  versus publicity, 169
  in telling community about
    civic marketing, 153, 157
Aggressiveness, 112–113
Alliances, forming, 39–40
Alumni magazine, writing for, 58
Article reprint/clip, 218
Articles
  brainstorming for ideas for, 59
  getting guidelines for, 59
  getting published, 60–61
  making informative, 61–62
  in marketing efforts, 62
  submitting query letters for, 61
  writing, 56–57
Atmosphere, creating, with customer service, 29–32
Attribution, 218
Audience, speaking to, 72–74
Audiotapes, 96
Awards, 83–84, 162

B
Background, 218
Bacon's Media Directories, 193
Bags as promotional materials,
  18–19
Baldrige, Malcolm, National
  Quality Award, 34–35
Bartering, 47–48, 147–148
Beat, 218
Biographer, hiring, 24
Board of Advisors, 39–44
  agenda for meeting of,
    42–43, 51
  brainstorming sessions of,
    43–44
  definition of, 41
  sample letter for, 50
  selecting professionals for,
    41–43

as source of referrals, 43
Booklets, writing, 63
Books, writing, 63, 64–66
Brainstorming, 116–117
  for article ideas, 59
  in selecting logo, 12–13
  sessions of, with Board of
    Advisors, 43–44
Brand, creating distinctive,
  129–132
Broadcast story, creating credi-
  bility through, 168–169
Brochures as promotional mate-
  rials, 18–19
B-Roll, 97, 218
Business cards, selection of dis-
  tinctive, 14–15
Businesses
  imitating top, 32–34
  reasons for engaging in civic
    marketing, 146–149
Businesses trends, writing
  about, 59
Business journals, writing for, 58
Byline, 57, 218

C
Cachet, creating, 122–124
Camera, use of, to record work-
  related events, 21–22, 23–24
Cash flow, increasing, through
  bartering, 48
Cause-related marketing,
  146–147. *See also* Civic marketing
Celebrity endorsement for press
  release, 181
Celebrity status, leveraging,
  93–94
Charities, advantages to, and
  civic marketing, 147–148
Chutzpah, 116
Civic marketing, 143–164
  benefits from, 145
  employee participants in,
    153–155
  newsletters in, 161
  planning in, 156–164
  proclamation in, 161
  reasons businesses engage in,
    146–149
  time frame in, 160–164
Class, holding, 80–81

Clients, listening to, 31
Clipping service, subscribing
  to, 198
Columns, writing, 59
Community-access TV show,
  producing, 163
Community involvement, 182
Company foyer, lobby, or win-
  dows, use of, as showcase of
  efforts, 163–164
Company name, finding perfect,
  4–5
Complementary causes, con-
  tributing to, 143–155
Complementary fit, finding,
  149–152
Contest, entering or establishing,
  81–84
Controversy, use of, in adver-
  tising, 184–185
Conversation piece, creating, 125
Corporate image, creation of, 4,
  11–12
Credibility, creating, 168–169
Crisis situation, confronting,
  206–207
Cross promotions, 46–47
Customer needs and desires,
  33–35
Customer service, 29–32, 35

D
Demonstration, holding, 80–81
Direct marketing through e-mail,
  102–103
Dressing
  for impressions, 25–35
  for TV interviews, 205

E
Editorial calendar, use of, in
  timing pitch, 192
E-mail, direct marketing
  through, 102–103
Employees, participation of, in
  your civic marketing,
  153–155
Envelopes, selection of distinc-
  tive, 14
Exhibitions, speaking opportuni-
  ties offered by, 72–73
Expertise, 79–85, 183
External writing markets, 58

219

SEND US YOUR
MARKETING SECRETS!

Do you have a great marketing idea you're eager to try? Have you used a marketing trick that's reaped great success—or simply know of one that really worked? Do you have exciting and creative visual samples of your business cards, stationery, logos, and so on? Let us know! We would like to hear all about them, and may even possibly use these ideas in a sequel. Please send your information to the authors, c/o Adams Media Corporation, 260 Center St., Holbrook, MA 02343.

Other books by Debbi J. Karpowicz include *I Love Men in Tasseled Loafers,* Quinlan Press, 1988. Other small business resources from Nancy Michaels include *How to Be a Big Fish in Any Pond—Memorable Marketing Strategies for Micro-Business and Entrepreneurs; Media Madness—How to Capture the Ongoing Interest of the Press;* and *A to Z Visibility—26 Keys to Unlock Your Visibility in the Marketplace.*

Check them out on the Web at www.worksmartproductions.com.